Fo...

in

Love & Spirit

R & N

July '04

WHISKY
CLASSIFIED

◆

DAVID WISHART

WHISKY
CLASSIFIED

CHOOSING SINGLE MALTS BY FLAVOUR

PAVILION

To Doreen With Love

First published in Great Britain in 2002 by
PAVILION BOOKS LIMITED

A member of **Chrysalis** Books plc

64 Brewery Road
London N7 9NT
www.chrysalisbooks.co.uk

Text © David Wishart 2002
Design and layout © Pavilion Books Ltd. 2002

The moral right of the author has been asserted

Designed by Bernard Higton
Map illustrations Gill Tomblin

A CIP catalogue record for this book is available
from the British Library

ISBN 1 86205 527 0

Repro by Classicscan Pte. Ltd., Singapore
Printed in Singapore by Kyodo Printing
Company Limited

This book can be ordered direct from the
publisher. Please contact the Marketing
Department. But try your bookshop first.

CONTENTS

INTRODUCTION

Many books have been written about whisky, but *Whisky Classified* is the first to attempt to *classify* single malt whiskies by their flavour. The subject of whisky is fraught with myths and jargon, to an extent that can be very off-putting for the newcomer. This book aims to answer some of the common questions, to guide the reader through the detail to a point at which it should be possible to enjoy drinking single malt whiskies and to understand something about them and their taste.

The difference between a blended whisky and a single malt whisky is the first source of confusion. Blended whisky has by far the larger market, yet a blend usually has no provenance: it is a recipe for a mixture, known only to the master blender. If it is described as "Scotch" then it must have been produced in Scotland, but this does not mean it relates to any particular distillery. The proportion of malt whisky in a blend is usually a closely guarded secret, because some contain more malt whisky than others. However the bulk of most blends is made up of grain whiskies, which can be produced on an industrial scale in the large quantities needed to sustain international sales.

Whereas a blend is a branded recipe for a mixture, each single malt whisky, *by definition*, originates from one Scottish distillery, a *single* source, hence the use of the word "single". It must also be made exclusively from malted barley, and matured in seasoned oak cask for at least three years. When you drink a single malt whisky, you share the heart and soul of the people who made it, and you can relate both to those people and to the place in which it was made. Unlike other potable spirits, all the malt whiskies that are currently available were distilled in the last millennium, and this will remain broadly true until after 2010. This book considers why whiskies are matured in oak casks, the importance of ageing, and the effect ageing has on flavour.

It is reasonable to assume that if you are reading this book then you are already interested in drinking whisky. Your first discovery will probably have been a single malt whisky that tasted different from any other whisky you had ever drunk before. Your next step might be to collect some contrasting malts, so that you can demonstrate your first discovery to your friends. Later on, you might seek out particular editions, because distilleries now offer special "finishes", which enhance the character of their malts by increasing their complexity – this is precisely the antithesis of a blend. When you are really hooked, you will probably want to visit your favourite distilleries and sample their whiskies from individual casks – you might even start buying single malt whiskies at cask strength that have not been diluted or chill-filtered.

The aim of this book is to help you navigate through this fascinating subject and to provide some shortcuts along the way. The taste of malt whiskies is described using a standardized flavour profile, which was developed by analysing hundreds of tasting notes. This provides an objective way of comparing the whiskies' distinctive and compelling characters. It is the approach that is instinctively used by the malt master to choose casks for vatting, or by the master blender to select whiskies for blending, though obviously not to the same degree of precision. However, the flavour profile in this book offers sufficient guidance on *flavour at a glance* for the average whisky drinker, and much help for the novice. Lastly, malt whiskies that are broadly similar in terms of their flavour are grouped together, so that if you find one that you really like then others of a similar character can be readily identified.

Some writers have attempted to compile "quality" league tables of malt whiskies by awarding them marks out of ten, according to taste. They assess the whiskies subjectively in terms of their personal flavour preferences, which are usually based on complexity, character and balance. However, if your preference happens to be for a lighter, aperitif style of malt whisky then such quality assessments are not very helpful; they are also unpopular in the industry, especially amongst distillers whose malt whiskies are not ranked very highly according to these criteria. Therefore, this book does not attempt to rank single malt whiskies on "quality", but rather to classify them by their flavour.

This book sets out to explain the taste of single malt whiskies: why they taste different from each other, their character, and their provenance. When you have found one that you like, experiment with other malt whiskies from the same flavour group. This book will help you to assemble a representative collection of single malts that span the malt whisky flavour spectrum. You will then be ready to host your own malt whisky tastings with friends, to discuss their flavours, their differences, where they come from, who makes them, and how they are made. Help is given with the pronunciation of names, which can be especially difficult if they are Gaelic.

I invite you to share in Scotland's wonderful whisky heritage, to broaden your experience of our great malt whiskies, and to learn about the people who made them and how they were made.

Always remember that the whisky you drink today was hand-crafted and laid down a decade or more ago by dedicated people confident in the knowledge that the fruits of their labour would be appreciated by generations to come. I hope you will enjoy the journey.

David Wishart

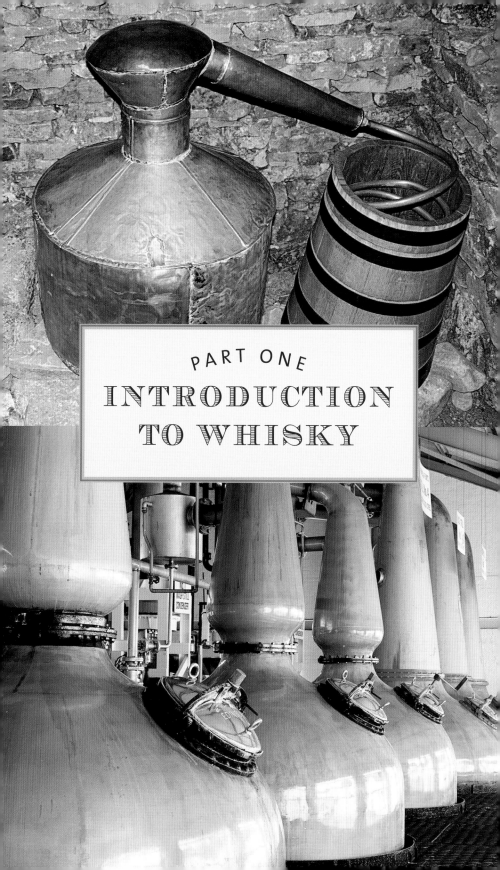

PART ONE

INTRODUCTION TO WHISKY

History of Whisky

The process of distillation was probably discovered by the Egyptians and Chinese for the extraction of perfumes, and adapted by monks in Europe around the eleventh century for the distillation of wine to produce its spirit. The practice spread rapidly as the hedonistic effects of *aqua vitae* "the water of life" became known. In more northern climates, unsuitable for growing grapes, the process was adapted for distilling fermented cereals, especially barley. A form of whisky was being distilled in Ireland by the twelfth century, and the practice was probably introduced to Scotland by Irish monks.

We know that St Columba travelled from Ireland and landed on Iona in AD 563, an important date in Scotland's religious history. The Scottish island of Islay, close to Iona, has a long tradition of producing malt whisky and strong historical connections with Ireland through the common language of Gaelic. Its western tip is roughly equidistant from the Giant's Causeway in Co. Antrim and Kintyre on the Scottish mainland, so it would have

been a simple matter to take a primitive still to Islay by boat. Legend has it that an Irish giant jumped to Scotland with a cask of whisky on his back, and it is no coincidence that *aqua vitae* translates into the Gaelic "uisge beatha" in Scots and "usque baugh" in Irish.

The first recorded reference to whisky is in the Exchequer Rolls of Scotland for 1494, which list an order from King James IV for "eight bolls of malt to Friar John Cor of Lindores Abbey, with which to make *aqua vitae*". Following the dissolution of the monasteries in the sixteenth century, many monks put their skills to work as distillers of "uisge beatha" which was famous for its medicinal qualities. James Hogg, the Ettrick Shepherd, is reported to have said "If a body could find out the exac' proper proportion and quantity that ought to be drunk every day, and keep to that, I verily trow that he might leeve for ever, without dying at a', and that doctors and kirkyards would go oot o' fashion".

The task of distillation was initially performed by monks, but farmers were quick to acquire the new skills since it was, after all, their cereals that provided the principal ingredient and they doubtless enjoyed the product of their labours. By the sixteenth century, whisky distillation had become commonplace on farms throughout Scotland, and the process was refined by the development of the familiar pear-shaped pot still and the use of cold stream water for improved condensation of the spirit. It was in the sixteenth century that

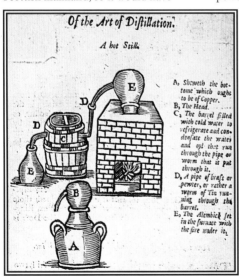

Early design for a primitive whisky still, including worm condenser.

The Highland Whisky Still *by Sir Edwin Landseer, 1829, depicts equipment used in illicit distillation.*

Scots Law first interfered with whisky production. In 1505 the Guild of Surgeon Barbers in Edinburgh was granted a monopoly for the production of *aqua vitae* for use as a medicine, and by the mid-sixteenth century prosecutions for infringement of their licence were commonplace as whisky had become a popular drink. The first tax on spirits was imposed in 1644, and commercial distillers were operating by the end of the seventeenth century.

Demand increased in the eighteenth century, especially when the Gin Act of 1736 imposed a tax on gin which did not apply to whisky. The official production of *aqua vitae* in Scotland rose from 100,000 gallons in 1708 to 275,000 gallons in 1738. It was at about this time that the term "uisge beatha" became corrupted, first to "usky" and then to "whisky".

It was commonplace in the eighteenth century for farms and large houses in Scotland to have their own still, which could legally be used to distil whisky for private consumption. In 1779 the size of private stills was reduced from 10 to 2 gallons, and Excise officers were empowered to confiscate and destroy larger stills. Two years later, private distillation was prohibited altogether, driving illicit distillers underground and more firmly establishing the commercial producers. The Wash Act of 1784 set lower Excise duty rates north of the "Highland Line" to encourage the illicit Highland distillers to become licensed. They were limited to one still of up to 20 gallons, and taxed at £1 per gallon of capacity a year. This encouraged a rapid growth of licensed distillers in the Highlands, and a further Act in 1785 was introduced to prohibit the export of Highland whisky. This resulted in a massive growth in licensed distilleries in the Lowlands which, despite paying

Queen Victoria with her gillie John Brown, at Balmoral. Their relationship aroused much speculation and inspired the film "Mrs Brown".

higher duty, had the advantage of exclusively selling their whiskies in the Scottish cities and in England.

In 1822, King George IV visited Edinburgh to attend a gala reception organized by Sir Walter Scott. The King repealed the prohibition on the wearing of tartan, which had been introduced after the rebellion of 1745. He declared a contraband malt whisky called "Glenlivet" to be his favourite whisky and directed that it be used as a toast at all Scottish ceremonial occasions.

Such was the demand for Glenlivet that extra supplies were urgently requisitioned from the Highlands. Elizabeth Grant, writing in her *Diary of a Highland Lady*, describes the Glenlivet that she sent to King George from

Rothiemurchus as "whisky long in the wood … mild as milk". This seems to be the earliest reference to the beneficial effects of maturing whisky in casks; however, it was definitely an upper class practice as the bulk of "uisge beatha" continued to be drunk straight from the still. Much of it must have been foul, for it was common to add honey, herbs and spices to conceal the taste and to drink it in fruit punches and hot toddies.

The royal romance with whisky continued through the next two generations, with Royal Brackla distillery being granted the first royal warrant in 1835 by William IV who proclaimed it to be his favourite whisky. Glenury Royal was another distillery to be patronized by William IV who was a friend of its founder, Captain Barclay. Sadly, this distillery is no longer open.

In 1848, the young Queen Victoria and her consort Prince Albert toured

Scotland. They visited many towns and villages and acquired a taste for all things Scottish, including whisky. Balmoral Castle was rebuilt to meet their requirements and became their summer residence, and so it has remained for most of the royal family that have followed, including Queen Elizabeth II. At the start of Queen Victoria's hunts at Royal Deeside, each guest would be given a bottle of whisky and whatever remained in it at the end of the day became the perquisite of his stalker. Queen Victoria made a general order that royal coaches should always travel with a bottle of whisky under the coachman's seat, for use in emergencies. Her patronage of distilleries was recognized by the award of a royal warrant to Lochnagar and a renewal of King William IV's warrant to Brackla.

The whisky industry flourished during Queen Victoria's reign, partly due to all things Scottish becoming popular in royal society. It was also helped by a Phylloxera plague in 1863, which devastated the vineyards of France and led English wine and brandy drinkers to turn to whisky. The quality and consistency of the whisky was unreliable, however, and it was possibly for this reason that the practice of blending was introduced. John Dewar and Arthur Bell, rival wine and spirit merchants of Perth, discovered that a more consistent product could be produced by blending several malt whiskies from different distilleries, and their whisky blends were launched in the 1850s. This was perhaps the first time that malt whiskies were classified by their flavour, the blender's art being to select a malt, or substitute one for another, according to its flavour and thereby maintain the balance and consistency of the brand.

At about the same time, a merchant called Andrew Usher hit on the idea of introducing grain whiskies to a blend. These are distilled from unmalted barley, wheat or maize, they are lighter than malts and are cheaper to produce using the continuous patent still that had been invented by Robert Stein in 1830 and improved by Aeneas Coffey, a former Exciseman. Others followed, and by the 1890s the industry was booming with new proprietary brands introduced by W.P. Lowrie, Charles Mackinlay, John Haig, John Walker, James Whyte and Charles Mackay, and James Buchanan, all of whom went on to become household names. So successful were they that they engaged foreign agents and began marketing their brands internationally. The most famous instance of this was Tommy Dewar's world tour of 1891–3, which resulted in 32 new agencies for Dewar's brands. As a result of this boom, existing distilleries expanded and many new ones were built. In the 1890s alone, 33 new distilleries were built, 21 of which were on Speyside. Stock in warehouses also increased massively, from 2 million gallons in 1892 to 90 million gallons by 1898. However, the whisky boom was not to last past the turn of the twentieth century.

The first shock was the bankruptcy in 1898 of a firm of blenders run by Robert and Walter Pattison. Aside from fraudulent accounting practises, the Pattisons had also resorted to selling grain whisky that contained colouring and very little else as their "Finest Glenlivet" blend. Pattisons collapsed, causing a slump in whisky prices and stock valuations; the Pattison brothers were tried for fraud and sent to prison. Demand for whisky also fell, due in part to the Boer War which interrupted

Above: *Whisky barrels at Wick waiting to be shipped.*

Below: *Lloyd George imposed punishing taxes on Scotch whisky.*

overseas trade, but also because of a general economic decline.

King Edward VII rejected whisky in favour of French wine and brandy, and fashions changed. War broke out between the whisky blenders and distillers as to what constituted *real* whisky. In 1905, Islington Borough Council successfully prosecuted two merchants for selling whisky "not of the nature, substance and quality demanded". That judgement went to appeal, and was eventually settled during World War I by the Immature Spirit Act of 1915 (as amended), which specified that whisky had to be matured in casks for a minimum of three years.

This rule remains in force today – a legislative shackle on the whisky industry that does not apply to the maturation of any other potable spirits. The 1915 Act was promoted by David Lloyd George, the teetotal Chancellor of the Exchequer, who declared drink to be a deadlier enemy in World War I than Germany and Austria. Having increased the distillers' licence fee in his 1909 Budget, Lloyd George used the 1915 Budget to increase the duty payable on whisky by a third. This was designed to switch consumption from whisky to beer, a policy that infuriated the Scotch whisky industry.

Distilleries were closed during World War I to preserve barley stocks for food, whisky exports were banned in 1917, and whisky duty was doubled in 1918 to increase war revenues. After the war, the distillers hoped to rebuild the industry, but were frustrated by a further increase in duty in the Budget of 1919. In the 1920s, the temperance movement gained sway in Britain, and the United States banned whisky imports and introduced prohibition.

Fortunately, US prohibition proved rather less effective than the temperance movement at suppressing whisky. Supplies of "Cutty Sark", a light, premium blend of whisky named after the fastest sailing ship of its day, were diverted to the US in the 1920s by Captain William McCoy, a bootlegger based in the Bahamas. Such was the popularity of his contraband whisky

that speakeasy patrons demanded the "real McCoy", an expression for "Cutty Sark" that subsequently entered the language on both sides of the Atlantic. Whisky was also legally imported into the US as medicine, "Laphroaig" and the blend "White Horse" being prescribed for medicinal purposes by American doctors during prohibition.

By 1924, there were only 84 distilleries in production, compared to 161 in 1899, but this was to fall further reaching a nadir in 1933 when only two malt whisky distilleries were operating. Production of whisky again stopped during World War II, and by 1945 the Scotch whisky industry had suffered 45 years of decline caused by three wars, US prohibition, temperance, taxation and hostile legislation. As the saying goes, things could only get better.

The 1960s was a time of construction, expansion and consolidation in the whisky industry. Many mothballed distilleries reopened, and others were rebuilt, extended or otherwise

Captain William McCoy smuggled Cutty Sark whisky into the USA during Prohibition, where it was dubbed the "real McCoy".

Above: An early poster for Johnnie Walker, with its distinctive square bottle first developed in the 1870s.
Below: This souvenir "sleeping" ice bucket celebrates the link between whisky and golf.

modernized. In 1958, Tormore and Glen Keith distilleries opened, the first to be built for nearly 60 years (since Glen Elgin, in May 1900). Regrettably, this period of reconstruction of distilleries also resulted in many of the industry's most beautiful Victorian buildings being lost. Processes such as malting barley, maturation, blending and bottling were centralized for greater efficiency, and the marketing departments became a driving force, at least in the successful operations.

There was much consolidation in the industry. United Distillers acquired a number of distilleries, eventually owning over 60, though it continued to keep several in mothballs only using them to mature other stock. It acquired a wine division within Grand Metropolitan, was consolidated into Diageo and merged with Guinness.

Other distilleries changed hands or were absorbed into groups, several being acquired by such major multi-nationals as Bacardi, Pernod Ricard and Suntory. Traditional skilled jobs, such as the stillman and maltster, were largely replaced by computerization, mechanization and the development of multi-skilled teams. In some instances these teams work two distilleries each on a six-month cycle. This has reduced the need for a large workforce.

Fearing for its independence in the face of acquisitions by the large multi-nationals, the directors of William Grant & Sons, who own Glenfiddich and Balvenie distilleries, decided in the 1960s to set aside some of their stock for sale internationally as a single malt whisky. This stroke of genius led to the revival of single malts which, throughout the 1980s and 1990s, grew in popularity. Sales of malt whiskies remain a small proportion of the total at under 15 per cent, but are growing as the market matures.

In 1975 the Scotch Malt Whisky Society was established by a group of enthusiasts, who hit upon the idea of buying individual casks collectively and bottling them for members. Membership of the Society is the goal of the connoisseur, because it gives the opportunity to experience the widest range of malt whisky flavours, from the idiosyncratic to the greats – the Society has always put much effort into tasting and selecting really great malt whiskies by there flavour.

WHISKY REGIONS

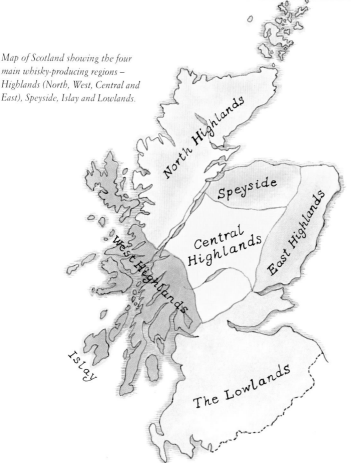

Map of Scotland showing the four main whisky-producing regions – Highlands (North, West, Central and East), Speyside, Islay and Lowlands.

The Scotch Whisky Association is the official trade organization for the whisky industry, responsible for representing it on national and international policy issues, for example, in policing the use of the term "Scotch" and in marketing. It categorizes distilleries according to four main whisky-producing regions in Scotland – Highlands, Lowlands, Islay and Speyside. This geographical split is difficult to justify today based on the number of distilleries now operating in each region: Highlands (31), Lowlands (3), Islay (7) and Speyside (45). Thus, while Islay is understandably singled out as a separate region, having seven operational distilleries, another six distilleries operating on other islands are classed within the Highland region, including Jura, which is closer to Islay than it is to the mainland.

The principal reason for this is that in the period 1784–1816, different Excise duty rates applied north and south of the "Highland Line". Campbeltown, which once had a thriving whisky industry of more than 32 distilleries, was officially excluded from the Highlands in 1785 and many of the producers were driven underground. Today there are only two distilleries

Cutting peat from an Islay moor.

operating in Campbeltown, namely Springbank and Glen Scotia, with plans advanced for Glengoyne to be restarted.

There has been a tradition of describing some whiskies as typically "Islay", "Highland", "Lowland" or "Speyside", and in some instances singling out particular malts as, for example, a "benchmark" or "definitive" Speyside, suggesting that malt whiskies can be differentiated by their geography. Speyside has the largest concentration of whisky distilleries in Scotland, due historically to the suitability of their isolated locations for illicit operation and for the quality of the water. Most draw their water from the surrounding mountain springs that feed the River Spey. The mountains are covered in peat and heather, lying thinly on granite and quartz. The rain falling on these hard crystalline rocks runs quickly to the distilleries and during the winter months it is very cold. The rainwater does not pick up minerals from such rocks and is typically soft, though peaty and acidic from passing through the heather peat. It is said that the best water for whisky is soft and flows through peat over granite, which exactly describes the Spey valley geology. The combination of suitable water sources, plentiful peat for the kilns and good supplies of local barley, naturally led to the establishment of the Speyside distilleries and influenced the character of their whiskies.

The Spey valley is home to the largest concentration of Scotch whisky distilleries.

A view of Islay, home to seven distilleries.

Nowadays, the water source is the main feature of a distillery that affects the flavour of the whisky, and even this is changing under EU regulations governing the purity of water in food and drink. With the introduction of coal and coke in the nineteenth century, and electric, gas and oil-fired kilns in the twentieth century, the dependence on peat-fired kilns to dry the barley diminished. Distillers were able to experiment with lighter peating, and indeed many have adapted their malts to a lighter, less peated style – examples are Bunnahabhain, Jura and Tobermory; while Clynelish, Springbank and Lagavulin have reduced the level of peat phenols in their malts in recent years. Also, most distillers now obtain their malted barley from commercial maltings, rather than malting it themselves in the traditional way, and most bottle their whiskies centrally, using a different water source from that of the distillery. The use of wooden washbacks (see page 21) has given way to stainless steel ones, though many distilleries continue to use larch or pine washbacks in an effort to preserve the original character of their whisky. Cask maturation also plays a more important part in determining the flavour of the matured whisky, with many producers using first-fill sherry casks or special cask "finishes".

It is therefore difficult to avoid the conclusion that the geographical classification of whisky has largely lost its significance. It is really only useful if you are trying to find a distillery on the map, perhaps with a view to visiting it. The map on pages 42–3 shows about 40 distilleries that welcome visitors and facilities are detailed under each distillery's entry in the A–Z section of this book. If you are a visitor to Scotland you should try to visit at least one distillery to soak up the ambience of an industry that has grown from the crofts to the continents, and which is unambiguously associated with the word "Scotch".

MAKING WHISKY

The ingredients of malt whisky are very simple – barley, peat, water and yeast. Brewers of real ale understand the importance of selecting good quality barley, and the same is

true for whisky – indeed, the first stage of whisky-making is beer-making. Good Scottish barley with a high starch content, like *Golden Promise*, is considered best, even though newer varieties, such as *Chariot*, yield more alcohol. Barley should also be dry, plump and free from mould and insects.

Before barley can be used, it must first be malted, a process by which the starch in the barley grains is modified to produce sugar maltose for conversion to alcohol during fermentation. The first stage is to soak the barley in water for two to three days. This causes the barley to swell and start germinating. Little rootlets and a shoot form on each barley grain and the grain becomes soft and sticky. During this time, the barley is turned regularly to keep it cool, while the starch in the grains turns to sugar and the natural enzyme diastase is released. The traditional method of turning the "green malt" is on a malting floor using a wooden shovel called a "shiel" and this method is still used at a handful of traditional distilleries. However, it is labour intensive and has been largely replaced by specialist maltings where the germinating barley is turned mechanically in large drums.

Germination continues for about a week, by which time the green malt is now laden with natural sugars from which the alcohol will be produced. Germination is halted by drying the barley, either over a kiln

or by using hot air, and, where peat is used to fuel the kiln, this imparts the distinctive smoky flavour to the whisky. After about 24 hours in the kiln the green malt has become dried malt, which is crisp and sweet.

Before the Industrial Revolution, the barley was always roasted over a peat fire, hence the location of early distilleries close to plentiful supplies of peat and water. Gradually peat was replaced by coke, and it became possible to produce lighter whiskies. Following the introduction of electricity in the mid-twentieth century, some distilleries discontinued the use of fossil fuels altogether, drying their barley in hot air to produce "unpeated" whiskies. Glengoyne and Auchentoshan are examples of distilleries that produce unpeated whiskies.

Most distilleries now obtain their malted barley from commercial maltings where it can be prepared to

Turning the barley during germination.

order. This includes specifying the amount of peat to be used in the drying process, thereby maintaining the consistency of peat flavours in the distillery's products. It is also possible to vary the amount of peat in different batches and thus produce a range of whiskies of varying phenolic content, or degrees of peatiness.

At the distillery, the malted barley is stored in large hoppers ready for use. At the next stage the barley is cleaned in dressing machines and milled into a rough flour called grist. This grist is then mixed with hot water in a vessel called a mash tun, or with the liquor retained from previous mashings. The water dissolves the maltose sugars in the flour, and the resulting liquid called "wort" is drained off and cooled ready for fermentation. The spent grain remaining in the mash tun is usually supplied to farmers as cattle feed, and the distillers are justly proud of the fact that their waste products are recycled in this way. The wort is then fermented in large vessels

Stoking a kiln with peat to dry the barley.

called washbacks. These are traditionally made of wood, such as Oregon pine or Siberian larch, though some distilleries now use stainless steel washbacks which are easier to clean and more hygienic. Those that use wooden washbacks do so to preserve the character of their whiskies, because the wood harbours bacteria that are believed to enhance the flavour of the resulting wash. At least one distiller that experimented with stainless steel has since reverted to wooden washbacks.

Yeast is now added to the wort and fermentation begins. This is a turbulent part of the process, as the liquid froths and large amounts of carbon dioxide are emitted. Most washbacks are fitted with a revolving froth-cutter, without which the froth would overflow and be

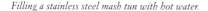

Filling a stainless steel mash tun with hot water.

The stillhouse at Bowmore distillery.

wasted, and in some distilleries this process is now computer-controlled. Another issue is whether or not to draw off the carbon dioxide using an extractor fan; however, this may reduce the character and strength of the wash.

During fermentation the yeast converts sugars in the wash into carbon dioxide and alcohol, which in turn reacts with acids from the malt to form esters and aldehydes that contribute the fruity and floral flavours to the spirit. For example, acetic acid reacts with ethanol to form ethyl acetate which smells like raspberries, and with amyl alcohol to form amyl acetate which smells like pineapples. A bacterial fermentation can also occur towards the end of the process, which reduces the acidity and adds more flavours. The scents that we associate with flowers and fruits are usually due to a combination of many different esters formed during fermentation, and over a hundred different esters have been identified in the chemical analysis of whisky.

The initial phase of fermentation is spectacular as the yeast cells multiply rapidly causing the wash to froth and bubble violently. After about two days it slows down and is stopped, though some producers allow it to continue for 60 hours or more to develop the "character" of the spirit by adding the flavours from the secondary bacterial fermentation. At this point the "wash" resembles a rough beer and contains 7–9 per cent alcohol. It is then pumped to the still house where it is distilled twice or, at a few distilleries, three times – hence the term triple distilled.

The first distillation takes place in the larger "wash" stills, where the alcohols, esters, aldehydes and acids are separated from the yeast, other impurities and most of the water. The process commences when the temperature within the wash still approaches the boiling point of water. As the fermented liquid is heated, the alcohols in the wash vaporize and rise up the still and over the neck, or "lyne arm". Traditional condensers consist of a copper coil or "worm" immersed in a tank of cold water, while modern condensers utilize hollow plates suspended in a continuous flow of cold water. Here the vapours condense into a rough, oily liquid called "low wines", containing about 17 per cent alcohol.

This is then pumped into a smaller "low wines" or spirit still where it is further refined by a second distillation. The stillman exercises much more control in this second distillation as only the "middle cut", or heart of the spirit, is collected. This occurs as the spirit flows through a spirit safe, introduced by the Excise in 1823 to allow the stillman to observe, assess and measure the density and quality of the flowing spirit. The strongest early spirit, called "foreshots", includes impurities and is collected and combined with the next batch of low wines for re-distillation. When the flow of spirit reaches the required strength and quality, the stillman diverts it to the "spirit receiver". This involves considerable skill, as the resulting quality of the final whisky will be influenced by how soon the stillman begins to "cut" the spirit run for collection. Towards the end of the run, the temperature in the still rises and various oily compounds called "feints" are vaporized. As these would spoil the flavour of the whisky, they are collected with the foreshots to be re-distilled with the next batch of low wines. The stillman thus takes only the "middle cut" from the flow of spirit, and it is only this clear new spirit, containing about 60–70 per cent alcohol, that is pumped to the filling store to be cooled and "filled" into oak casks for maturation.

The quality of the spirit is tested in the spirit safe.

At a few distilleries there is a third distillation, involving an intermediate still, the purpose of which is to produce a lighter whisky by removing most foreshots, feints and heavier alcohols before the final distillation in the spirit still. The size and shape of the still also contribute to the flavour of the whisky, due to the relative exposure to copper which catalyses reactions that, for example, convert aldehydes produced during fermentation into acids, alcohols and esters, and remove some undesirable feints. Smaller stills offer a greater exposure to copper and therefore encourage these reactions.

The traditional method of heating stills contributes indirectly to the exposure of their copper interiors. Stills that are heated from below by direct flame fires, quickly build up deposits of burnt solids on the interior and these need to be removed. This is done by "rummagers", which are heavy chains that are turned inside the stills to dislodge any burnt solids and burnish the copper. The process of rummaging increases the exposure of the wash to copper and thereby enhances the flavour of the spirit. Whereas most

A cooper mantains the oak casks prior to filling.

distilleries now heat their stills using steam coils or plates, Macallan reverted to direct flame heating after experimenting with steam, in the belief that direct flame heating and rummaging yield a better spirit.

The shape of the still is also very important to the final product, and when stills are renewed they are usually copied faithfully from the originals, including any bumps and dents, in order to maintain the character of the whisky. Tall-necked stills produce a finer, lighter spirit by causing the heavier vapours to condense before reaching the swan neck and to fall back as "reflux" to be evaporated again. Shorter stills allow more of the heavy compounds to pass over the lyne arm and therefore yield a fuller, richer spirit. Some stills incorporate a "boil ball" in the neck, which helps to partially cool the vapours so that the heavier volatiles

fall back as reflux. Wash purifiers and reflux condensers are also used for this purpose, as they condense the heavier vapours on the lyne arm, returning them as liquids to the still and thereby allowing only the lightest vapours to reach the condenser. This produces a lighter, more delicate spirit.

The process of maturing whisky in oak casks is relatively new, having only been introduced on a large scale from the mid-nineteenth century. Prior to that, practically all whisky was sold straight from the still at 60–70 per cent alcohol by volume. However, it was known that when whisky is stored in barrels that had previously been used for sweet wines, sherry or port, it becomes smoother and more flavoured. This process has developed into a fine art at distilleries such as Macallan, which matures all its malt whiskies in Spanish oak casks that are specially selected in Jerez, having previously been used to mature dry oloroso sherry for about two years.

Most malt whiskies are matured in casks that have previously been used for whisky, sherry or bourbon. In 1915, it became law in the United Kingdom for all whisky to be matured in oak casks for a minimum of three years before it can be called Scotch. This is in contrast to most other spirits for which no period of maturation is required by law.

, The type and size of oak cask used for maturation is very important. American oak has a tighter, harder grain than European oak and is therefore less porous. This means that there is generally less interaction between the whisky and the wood of an American oak cask, so that more of the character of the spirit is retained. Oak trees grow faster in Spain and therefore the grain is more porous. Spanish casks are usually selected from those that previously held sherry or port; in some cases they are carefully prepared with a particular sherry, such as Macallan's dry oloroso, to combine the flavours of the sherry with those of the whisky and thus add to its complexity. Sometimes they are prepared using Pedro-Jimenez Sherry, which is dark and sweet and therefore conveys more deep gold colour and sweet sherry flavour. Whiskies matured in former sherry casks are affected early on by the sherry that has seeped into the wood, whereas it is only in later years that the wood character begins to transfer to the whisky. On the other hand, when a cask has been filled with whisky for a third or fourth time, any sherry flavour or wood character will largely be spent, so that the flavour of the spirit will be modified to a much lesser extent. Such "refill" casks are mostly used to mature whisky that is intended for blending.

Although the casks are carefully sealed to prevent leakage, the oak is porous and there is therefore a loss of about 2 per cent of the spirit each year due to evaporation. This means that in 8 years of maturation, about 15 per cent of the whisky will be lost through evaporation; and after 20 years the volume can be reduced by a third or more. This is called the "angel's share", and explains the delightful aroma of maturing spirit that emanates from the warehouses. What other industry is required by law to store its entire output for several years, utilizing acres of warehousing space that requires monitoring and security, during which time a significant proportion of the stock simply evaporates into the air?

Stillman's testing kit – hydrometer, thermometer and sample jar.

Drawing a glass of whisky direct from the cask.

It is hardly surprising that whisky distillers place great emphasis on the unique qualities and flavours that are added during cask maturation, especially for those whiskies that are aged the longest.

Whisky is traditionally matured and gently mellowed in low, stone built, earth floored "dunnage" warehouses, where the casks are only stacked up to three high. If these warehouses are situated by the sea, the damp salty air permeates the casks, thereby imparting a salty note to the maturing whisky. Inland warehouses can have a more disruptive effect on the maturation process, due to the wider variations in temperature. It is normal for a black fungus that lives off evaporating alcohol, the *champignon ivrogne*, to grow on the walls of dunnage warehouses and even spread to the nearby trees. Look out for this on your visit to a distillery – if you do not see a blackened warehouse, this is an indication that their whiskies are being matured elsewhere. In modern warehouses, casks can be stacked twelve high, temperatures are controlled, and there is less air circulation. This can adversely affect the maturing whisky, and many distilleries use a combination of both types of warehouse.

Some distillers have recently introduced new "finishing" or double-wood processes that impart additional flavours during the final stages of maturation. The whisky is removed from conventional casks after the normal period of 10–15 years, and transferred to newer casks that are specially prepared with a fortified wine such as sherry or port, or a spirit such as cognac or calvados. These methods were partly introduced because of the scarcity of sherry casks, and are used sparingly for the last 9–12 months of maturation.

In 1996, Glenmorangie introduced its range of special "wood finishes", utilizing casks that had previously contained port, madeira or sherry; more recently, Malaga wine and Côte de Nuits Burgundy wood finishes have been added to their range. Glendronach, Glenfarclas and others have moved towards Macallan's approach, using sherry casks in their maturation. Glenfiddich vat whiskies, aged at least 15 years in sherry casks, to produce a sherried "blend" of their own malts under their Solera brand. Glen Moray offer malts finished in

Display of sample bottles, essential for blending.

chenin blanc and chardonnay casks, their advertising posing the question "are we talking white wine or single malt?" These special finishes also provide a new marketing angle that is intended to make the whiskies appeal more directly to wine and cognac drinkers.

The whisky industry has been analysing, testing and recording malt whiskies for well over a century, ever since it was discovered that several different malt whiskies could be mixed to create a smoother, more consistent, whisky blend. The result, it is argued, is smoother than any of the constituent malts, and regular buyers of a blend know what to expect. The truth is that large-scale production of blends can only be achieved by using a large proportion of grain whiskies, which can be produced on an industrial scale, and by substituting one malt whisky for another if need be, thereby avoiding the trap of being tied to particular distilleries having finite supplies.

The skill of the master blender is to taste, or rather "nose", a large range of whiskies and blend a selection of them together to maintain the flavour of his brand. The master blender's records traditionally take the form of a large array of sample bottles, and the whole business of blending is shrouded in the mystique of skills passed down from master to apprentice. All this is done in the name of consistency, because it is supposed that once you have found a whisky blend that you like, you will continue to buy it and drink it, and that brand will become part of your lifestyle.

A collector's edition of The Macallan, supplied in a decanter and presentation box.

By comparison with a blend, a single malt whisky originates from one Scottish distillery. By its age, you know roughly when it was distilled. Sometimes the year of distillation is stated explicitly, but more usually the bottle will carry a statement such as "10 years old". This does not mean that the whisky was distilled exactly 10 years ago, because the age statement has, by law, to be the *minimum* age of the whisky in the bottle. It is quite common, for example, to marry casks of different ages but which are at least 10 years old, to produce a single malt that is described as "10 years old". A key skill is that of cask selection, and the process of marrying the contents of different casks in a large vat for several weeks or months before it is bottled. Sometimes a particularly good cask of whisky may be selected and bottled at cask strength by the Master Blender or Distillery Manager to be sold as a special version.

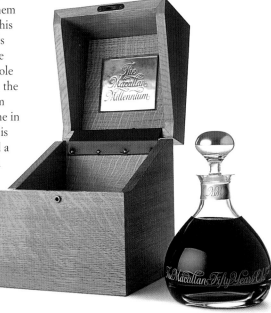

WHISKY FLAVOURS

The standard malt whisky flavour profile used in this book has been developed from a wide review of hundreds of malt whisky tasting notes. Several current books on malt whisky and distillers' tasting notes were reviewed, and a vocabulary of over 400 aromatic and flavour adjectives and nouns used to describe the aroma and flavour of malt whiskies was compiled (see pages 218–19).

The starting point for evaluating this vocabulary was the Pentlands Flavour Wheel, developed in 1979 by chemists at the Pentlands Scotch Whisky Research Institute (now the Scotch Whisky Research Institute). This was a terminology that classified the flavours and aromas found in whisky around the hub of a wheel, under·14 headings: primary taste, mouthfeel, nasal, phenolic, feints, cereal, aldehydic, estery, sweet, woody, oily, sour, sulphury and stale.

While the Pentlands Flavour Wheel provided a useful reference for the assessment of spirit by the industry, it was difficult for consumers to interpret and so it was simplified in the 1980s by John Lamond and Aberlour Distillery into the Aberlour Tasting Wheel. This concept was developed further in 1997 by MacLean, Newton and Swan into a three-tier tasting wheel. The flavours are described in everyday terms under eight "cardinal aromatic groups", namely: winey, cereal, estery, floral, peaty, feinty, sulphury and woody.

For the flavour profile in this book, a representative malt whisky from each Scottish distillery was then scored according to whether or not notes corresponding to the eight cardinal aromatic groups were present. The representative malt whisky selected was normally the distillery's most popular expression, though in some cases the choice was not as straightforward. For example, in his *Malt Whisky Companion*, Michael Jackson reviews 27 versions of Springbank, 18 of Glenturret and 15 of Glen Grant. While his tasting notes are valuable as archival references – for such *collectable* malts are rarely seen outside auction rooms, where they command high prices – it is beyond the scope of this book to attempt to classify the entire range. Rather, the purpose of this book is to evaluate malt whiskies that are readily available in bars and supermarkets today, and are at affordable prices.

With this aim firmly in mind, a target malt whisky, which had been aged in casks for about 10–15 years, was selected for each distillery. Even this standard is difficult to maintain because, for

Pentlands Flavour Wheel.

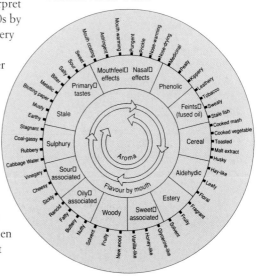

example, the main expressions from Lagavulin and Mortlach are matured for 16 years, while the very popular Auchentoshan Select and Loch Lomond malts carry no age statements. In the absence of a readily available 10 years old malt, the best-seller from each distillery was chosen for evaluation. It is important to note that each flavour profile in this book is for one malt whisky expression only, and cannot be extrapolated to others from the same distillery. There can be, and often is, considerable variation in the character of malts emanating from one distillery due to ageing, cask selection or special finishing.

In scoring the malts according to MacLean's eight cardinal aromatic groups, and from discussions with industry experts, it became apparent that some of the groups are too broadly constructed to reflect the diversity of different flavours found in the tasting notes. For example, the "peaty" group embraces smoky, peaty and pungent together with medicinal, iodine and seaweed notes, and whereas the former clearly derive from the use of peat to dry the barley and in the water, the latter can relate to water character or the maturation of whiskies near the sea. Although these flavours do often go together, for example as on Islay, this is more an accident of history and location than a causal link.

Likewise, sherried notes occur widely and yet MacLean's "winey" group also includes chocolate and nutty features related to the cask used in maturation. The different types and sizes of casks in which whiskies are matured give rise to a host of cask-related descriptions. For example, chocolate, nutty and vanilla are flavours derived from the type of oak used, whereas winey, port and sherried describe flavours introduced solely

by the previous contents of the cask.

For the flavour profile used in this book, a separate group has, therefore, been created for smoky and peaty notes, and similarly for winey and sherried notes, because both of these are important dimensions of flavour in their own right.

Sulphur flavours, which can be conveyed in poorly-malted barley or where sherry casks are sterilized by burning sulphur candles, rarely occur in the common malt whiskies on the market today. The sulphur group has, therefore, been excluded from the flavour profile. This is also true, to some extent, of the feints group, which includes undesirable flavours such as plastic, cheesy and sweaty that arise during the later stages of distillation and during maturation due to bung-cloth deterioration. Fortunately, such descriptions are rare in modern malt whiskies, thanks to the skill of the stillman when taking the middle cut, and of the malt master when selecting casks for vatting. However, the "feinty" group also includes desirable flavours such as tobacco, leather, hessian and honey, terms that occur quite widely in the description of popular malt whiskies. They have, therefore, been incorporated in the flavour profile as separate features, under the headings "tobacco" and "honey".

Lastly, there are liberal references in whisky literature to the sweetness (or sourness) and body of whiskies. Whether a whisky is sweet or dry is clearly a characteristic of its flavour that will determine its appeal, as with wine and other drinks. Body is more difficult, but can relate to the occasion on which a whisky might be drunk. For example, a lighter, aromatic whisky is more suitable as an aperitif, when the taste buds are fresh and receptive. By contrast, a full-bodied malt whisky with a big personality, such as a heavily-peated Islay malt, might be enjoyed as an after dinner drink with a strong cheese to complement it.

This book's standard flavour profile, therefore, comprises 12 flavour features into which the vocabulary of over 400 malt whisky adjectives and descriptive nouns has been grouped (see page 218–19). It has been presented at several scientific meetings, and was circulated with an industry survey, as a result of which some final adjustments were made. The flavour profile can be summarized as shown opposite.

The initial analysis, based solely on whether flavours were present or not in whiskies, proved to be too crude. This was because whisky writers and distillers differentiate quite carefully between pronounced features, light notes and hints. Throughout this book, these 12 flavour categories are, therefore, scored on a scale of 0–4 according to the intensity with which each feature is present in a whisky. The intensity rating is as follows:

0		Not present
1	●	Low Hints
2	●●	Medium Notes
3	●●●	Definite Notes
4	●●●●	Pronounced

Even so, whisky writers and distillers do not always agree on the intensity of the flavours they discern, so there is inevitably an element of judgement involved in determining the intensity ratings.

This book contains a flavour profile for each single malt whisky, in the following style:

Feature	Profile
●●	Body
●●	Sweetness
●●●	Smoky
●	Medicinal
	Tobacco
●●	Honey
●	Spicy
●	Winey
●	Nutty
●●	Malty
●	Fruity
●	Floral

This is the flavour profile for Highland Park 12 years old. In this case it shows that most of the flavours are present in the whisky, but none dominates – the most distinctive characteristic is smoke, a definite note that is sometimes referred to as the malt's "signature". Otherwise, the flavour profile is well-balanced and illustrates the complexity of this highly regarded single malt whisky.

Some readers will doubtless disagree with some of the flavour profiles contained in this book. But then, this is the essence of the pleasure of drinking malt whisky – to explore, evaluate and discover the delights of the barley and the wood, and to find that elusive bottle that unifies the components of flavour in exactly the right combination for your palate or for a special occasion.

FLAVOUR PROFILE

Body: its weight or fullness, influenced by the size of the still and the type of cask (light, through medium, to full-bodied).

Sweetness: sugars in the wash not converted during fermentation or by catalysis during distillation, and glucose extracted from new casks during maturation (dry, through medium-sweet, to sweet).

Smoky: where peat is used in kilning, and where the water flows through peat bogs (bonfires, burnt-heather, peaty, phenolic, pungent, kippery, mossy, earthy, fishing-nets, turfy).

Medicinal: salty, iodine flavours usually associated with seashore maturation (brine, iodine, menthol, salty ,sea-air, seaweed, turpentine).

Tobacco: feints introduced at distillation and during maturation, desirable in moderation (tea-chests, libraries, old-books, leather, leather-polish, car-seats, saddles, garden-sheds, hessian, musty).

Honey: released by catalysis of aldehydes during distillation or extracted from oak wood during maturation, especially new oak or casks prepared with bourbon (beeswax, heather-honey, mead, butterscotch, caramel, fudge, toffee, treacle, vanilla).

Spicy: extracted from oak wood during maturation, particularly where new wood is used (bay leaves, cedar, cinnamon, cloves, ginger, nutmeg, oaky, pepper, pine, sandalwood, tannic, woody).

Winey: flavours from what the casks contained before being filled with whisky, such as a special preparation of the cask with sherry, port or madeira to add a special finish (Chardonnay, Chenin Blanc, fino sherry, grapey, liqueurish, madeira, oloroso, port, sherry).

Nutty: mainly oak lactones extracted from casks during maturation, especially European oak, or fatty acids formed by bacterial growth during fermentation (almonds, hazelnuts, oily, walnuts, buttery, chocolate, creamy).

Malty: characteristics of the malt not removed by kilning or yeast by fermentation, usually showing in immature whiskies (barley, biscuits, cereal, grain, mashy, mealy, cooked-veg, malt-extract, husky, burnt-toffee, cake, roasted-coffee, liquorice, toasted, baking, yeasty).

Fruity: higher alcohols, aldehydes and esters formed at fermentation, by catalysis during distillation, and by reactions with oak wood during maturation (citric, estery, lemony, limey, oranges, tart, melons, peaches, pear-drops, strawberries, sweet-shop, stewed-apples, Christmas-pudding, fruit-cake, dried-fruit, raisins, sultanas, bubble-gum, solvent).

Floral: esters and aldehydes formed during fermentation and by reactions with oak wood during maturation (aromatic, fragrant, honeysuckle, perfumed violets, sugared-almonds, greenhouse, mint, sherbet, cut-barley, grassy, leafy, sappy, botanical, hay-like, heathery, herbal, meadows).

WHISKY TYPES

Having scored the malt whiskies on the flavour profile they can more readily be compared. Two malt whiskies that have exactly the same flavour profile, correctly scored, can be considered to be the same or similar in terms of their flavour. Some whisky *connoisseurs* would argue that this is not the case, and that every malt whisky is unique. While this is clearly true if their features are analysed to the utmost degree of refinement, it is not necessarily very helpful. For the purposes of better understanding *types* of people, plants, animals, insects, etc it is usually helpful to *classify* them – indeed language is a means of classifying and hence describing everything we encounter. The same it true of whisky, particularly from the consumer's point of view, as classification leads to a better understanding of how one product compares with another and, therefore, what to try next.

This, then, is an attempt to classify single malt whiskies according to their *flavour* as opposed to where they are made, or who makes them, or how they are sold. The standard flavour profile was scored for each whisky, and these profiles were then used to classify 86 malt whiskies using a scientific method known as "cluster analysis", originally developed in the biological sciences to describe the relationships between plants and animals. Put simply, the method groups malt whiskies that have *broadly* the same scores on all twelve flavour features, into the same clusters. The result is that all the whiskies in a cluster are similar in terms of their flavour profiles, while the clusters are differentiated by one or more of the flavour features.

In order to validate this system of classification, it was sent to all the distillers and to other industry experts, and published by the Scotch Malt Whisky Society in one of their newsletters. Many useful comments and some criticisms were received. Of those that replied, over 90 per cent thought that the approach was a reasonable one, yet needed further refinement. All the criticisms were carefully reviewed, in particular where respondents thought that a comparison was wrong or that certain malt whiskies were in the wrong cluster. The flavour profiles were revised in the light of these observations. The flavour profile was broadened to the present 5-point scale, described in the previous section, and additional sources of tasting notes were reviewed, including the distillers' own tasting notes, where these were available.

The cluster analysis was repeated on the revised scores and several different cluster levels were considered. The one that accords most closely with the industry survey is the 10-cluster grouping shown on page 33.

Cluster A (Full-bodied, medium-sweet, pronounced sherry with fruity, spicy, malty notes and nutty, smoky hints): Balmenach, Dailuaine, Dalmore, Glendronach, Macallan, Mortlach, Royal Lochnagar

Cluster B (Medium-bodied, medium-sweet, with nutty, malty, floral, honey and fruity notes): Aberfeldy, Aberlour, Ben Nevis, Benrinnes, Benromach, Blair Athol, Cragganmore, Edradour, Glenfarclas, Glenturret, Knockando, Longmorn, Scapa, Strathisla

Cluster C (Medium-bodied, medium-sweet; fruity, floral, honey, malty notes and spicy hints): Balvenie, Benriach, Dalwhinnie, Glendullan, Glen Elgin, Glen Ord, Glenlivet, Linkwood, Royal Brackla

Cluster D (Light, medium-sweet, low or no peat, with fruity, floral, malty notes and nutty hints): An Cnoc, Auchentoshan, Aultmore, Cardhu, Glengoyne, Glen Grant, Mannochmore, Speyside, Tamdhu, Tobermory

Cluster E (Light, medium-sweet, low peat, with floral, malty notes and fruity, spicy, honey hints): Bladnoch, Bunnahabhain, Glenallachie, Glenkinchie, Glenlossie, Glen Moray, Inchgower, Loch Lomond, Tomintoul

Cluster F (Medium-bodied, medium-sweet, low peat; malty notes and sherry, honey, spicy hints): Ardmore, Auchroisk, Deanston, Glen Deveron, Glen Keith, Glenrothes, Old Fettercairn, Tomatin, Tormore, Tullibardine

Cluster G (Medium-bodied, sweet, low peat and floral notes): Isle of Arran, Dufftown, Glenfiddich, Glen Spey, Miltonduff, Speyburn

Cluster H (Medium-bodied, medium-sweet, with smoky, fruity, spicy notes and floral, nutty hints): Balblair, Craigellachie, Glen Garioch, Glenmorangie, Oban, Old Pulteney, Strathmill, Tamnavulin, Teaninich

Cluster I (Medium-light, dry, with smoky, spicy, honey notes and nutty, floral hints): Bowmore, Bruichladdich, Glen Scotia, Highland Park, Isle of Jura, Springbank

Cluster J (Full-bodied, dry, pungent, peaty and medicinal, with spicy, tobacco notes): Ardbeg, Caol Ila, Clynelish, Lagavulin, Laphroaig, Talisker

Readers who are familiar with malt whiskies may recognize the two extremes of strongly sherried malts (Cluster A) and the heavily peated, mainly Islay malts (Cluster J). Adjacent to these polar benchmarks are the lightly sherried (clusters B and C) and lightly peated (clusters H and I) malts, with the light-bodied, floral and malty clusters, including four largely unpeated groups (clusters D–G) falling in the middle.

The 10 clusters can be combined into broader groupings (see below), which can be helpful when selecting 6 or 4 sample whiskies for tasting. The cluster of pungent, peaty Islay malts (J) is most distinctive, being maintained as a separate group to the end of the analysis, with the "sherries" of clusters A–C the next most distinctive, and clusters H–I separated as a group of well-balanced malts showing more complexity with no dominant features.

10 CLUSTERS		6 CLUSTERS		4 CLUSTERS	
Cluster	Sample whiskies	**Cluster**	Sample whiskies	**Cluster**	Sample whiskies
A	Mortlach	A	Dalmore		
B	Strathisla	B	Glenfarclas	A	Macallan
		C	Dalwhinnie	B	Aberlour
C	Glenlivet			C	Balvenie
D	Auchentoshan	D	Glen Grant		
		E	Glen Moray	D	
E	Glenkinchie			E	Glengoyne
				F	Bunnahabhain
F	Tomatin	F	Deanston	G	Glenrothes
		G	Speyburn		Glenfiddich
G	Arran				
H	Oban	H	Old Pulteney	H	Glenmorangie
		I	Springbank	I	Highland Park
I	Bowmore				
J	Lagavulin	J	Ardbeg	J	Laphroaig

TASTING WHISKY

It is a curious fact that when we taste whisky we use our nose far more than our mouth or tongue. Taste is a combination of the primary impression on the tongue supplemented by aromas detected by the nose, the nose being far more sensitive than the tongue. It has been estimated that for every taste bud on the tongue there are 10,000 taste receptors in the nose. That is why master blenders "nose" their whiskies rather than taste them, and when they are working they seldom drink any whisky at all.

While it can be instructive to evaluate whiskies simply by nosing them, for those of us who enjoy drinking whisky this is not exactly fun. But it can be a good discipline to begin a tasting session by pouring 5 or 6 malt whiskies into separate glasses and nosing them all before starting to drink any of them. The issue of what whiskies to choose for a tasting and the order in which they should be nosed and tasted is discussed later.

First, select the correct type of glass. The standard cut-glass whisky tumbler is not the ideal shape for nosing whiskies. The nosing glass used in the whisky industry is tulip shaped like a sherry glass with a narrow mouth and has graduations marked on the side. The narrow mouth is important for containing the aroma that rises from the whisky, so that when we nose it we get the maximum fragrance. For the same reason it is helpful to cover the mouth of the glass with a watch glass cover or lid that prevents the aromas from escaping, but it would be pedantic to regard these as essential. In the absence of proper nosing glasses, use small, tulip shaped wine glasses.

The next issue is the strength of the whisky to nose and taste, for it will be evident that not all malt whiskies are supplied at the same alcoholic strength. Although the majority are bottled at 40%, others are 43%, 46% and cask

strength 55-60%.
Incidentally, all whiskies that are bottled below cask strength will have been reduced by the addition of water at bottling, and it is fair to ask the distiller what water was used – it is not always the same source as the distillery.

In order to make a fair comparison between different whiskies, they should be nosed at the same alcoholic strength, and the industry standard is 20% alcohol by volume. This may not be popular with those who do not approve of adding water to their whisky. It is, however, an accepted fact that our taste receptors work best when not anaesthetised by alcohol, and 20% is a good strength at which the esters are fully released and can be most easily detected. Some people add much more water than whisky when tasting it, and this is also a good discipline especially if there is a need to remain sober. It is common in the West of Scotland to add lemonade to whisky and in America and other hot climes to add ice, but these and other mixers are best reserved for blends, rather than for malt whiskies because they modify the flavour.

For a nosing session, it is good practice to nose at full strength first and note any initial impressions. If you inhale too strongly you may feel nose prickle – this is caused by the alcohol vapour temporarily overloading your senses. When this happens, wait a moment and draw the whisky's aroma gently into your nose, trying to identify the individual fragrances. Next add enough still spring water to reduce the whisky to 20% and nose again. Standard nosing glasses have two graduations on the side, the lower one being the level to fill with whisky and the upper one being the level to top up with water. They correspond to equal volumes, and hence assume that the whisky has been bottled at 40%, so a slight adjustment is needed for a stronger whisky.

To taste the whisky, take a generous sip and note the body and mouth feel – is it smooth, creamy, oily or spirity. Move the whisky around your mouth checking the balance of sweet, sour, salty and bitter sensations detected by your tongue. Continue to check for fragrances through your nose, and estimate the strength of each flavour you detect using the flavour profile as a guide. As you swallow, note how long the flavours linger and what you taste after the whisky is gone – a long finish is considered desirable by connoisseurs.

Many people when starting to drink malt whiskies prefer light, aperitif styles, whereas experienced whisky drinkers are looking for depth, balance and complexity. Those who feel the urge to express their judgements by awarding marks-out-of-ten for quality are usually seeking balance and complexity, and their preferences do not necessarily coincide with those of beginners. A balanced whisky lacks any pronounced or dominating flavours, but presents a combination that often appears sequentially like peeling away the layers of an onion. This is why whisky writers usually describe the colour, nose, palate and finish in that order, which is the normal sequence in which a whisky is enjoyed.

We are now ready to start using the flavour profile to plan a tutored whisky tasting that illustrates the full variation in whisky styles. The first problem is that whereas the bottles usually need to be presented in line, the variations in flavour are far more complex than linear. The simplest model is two-dimensional, by which the degree of peat is represented in one direction and the degree of sherry or wine in another. It may be useful to select reference malts, such as the unpeated Glengoyne, the heavily peated Laphroaig and the strongly sherried Macallan. Most of the other malt whiskies fall somewhere between these poles (in the chart), such as Highland Park (above). If the chart is now

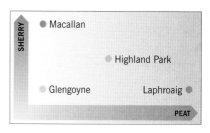

flattened into one dimension, the best representation places the lightest malt whiskies in the centre and work out to the polar extremes of cluster A to the left and cluster J to the right. When I host a *Whisky Classified* tutored tasting, I normally select six malt whiskies in this arrangement, such as those illustrated in the table below. They are normally arranged in line, but if space permits they can be placed on a square table in the centre of the room, arranged as in the chart below.

A	B – C	D – E	F – G	H – I	J
Dalmore	Aberlour	Auchentoshan	Deanston	Bowmore	Ardbeg
Glendronach	Balvenie	Bunnahabhain	Glenfiddich	Glenmorangie	Lagavulin
Macallan	Glenfarclas	Glengoyne	Glenrothes	Highland Park	Laphroaig
Mortlach	Strathisla	Glenkinchie	Speyburn	Springbank	Talisker

The whiskies at the centre are those with the lightest flavours, least modified by peating of the malted barley or maturation in European sherry casks. In a very broad sense, they allow the character of the spirit to show through, and should be tasted first. The tasting usually proceeds to the whiskies on the left, which have been more influenced by the choice of cask for maturation, and concludes with those to the right, which have been more influenced by the use of peat.

It can be noted that this is the reverse of chronological order, since the degree of peating of the barley is always the first decision, followed by mashing of the grist when peaty water can be introduced. Fermentation and distillation are next, when the character of the spirit is determined by the production processes used and the middle cut is taken. Maturation is the final stage, when cask selection is crucial to the texture and flavour, in some cases modified by special finishing. However, in guiding a tutored tasting there is no escaping the fact that cluster J should be tasted last, because these whiskies have the strongest peaty flavours and would spoil the palate for the more subtly flavoured malts in the centre. In conclusion, the whiskies in clusters B–C and H–I are those that frequently do well in tasting competitions, because they display balance and complexity with no particular flavours dominating.

Now that you have explored the delights and complexities of malt whisky, it is time to raise your glass and toast the people who made it. Making malt whisky is both an art and a science. There is also a lot of science in whisky making, from the maltster's role in ensuring the quality of the malted barley, the mashman's control of mashing and fermentation, the stillman's control of the distillation, and the malt master's selection of casks for filling. It's a team effort to craft a malt whisky, and when you drink it you share their soul and spirit. They are all vital to the quality of the final product.

It is also a commitment by them to the future, for the whisky produced today may not be drunk for a generation. It will lie quietly maturing in the cask for at least ten years before it is bottled and reaches you, by which time a new team may be working the distillery. It is thus a promise from one generation to the next, that the product of their labours past will be worthy of your future toast.

The most dramatic moment in the whole process, and one that is crucial to the quality and character of the whisky, is when the stillman takes the middle cut. Whisky production at most distilleries continues around the clock, therefore this is as likely to occur in the middle of the night as in a normal working day. So, I invite you to raise your glass and toast the stillman as he pursues his lonely craft on the night shift, in the knowledge that it will take a decade or more before his newly made spirit emerges from the cask as single malt whisky for us to enjoy.

Scotia's Gold

Raise a glass to the stillman's skill,
    alone in the night, he tends his still.
Charges the wash, brings to the boil,
    dewy beads form in a copper coil.

Starts at a trickle, then a flow,
    cloudy foreshots the first to show.
Checks for strength, clear of mist,
    crystal spirit o' coarse milled grist.

Spirit safe cranks, sounding the hour,
    seizes the essence o' barley flower.
Clear flows the run, pulses the heart,
    cuts the middle wi' his stillman's art.

Draught o' his craft, now bares its soul,
    character's formed in a tulip bowl.
Then raise your glass, my kindred host,
    wi' Scotia's gold, our worthy toast.

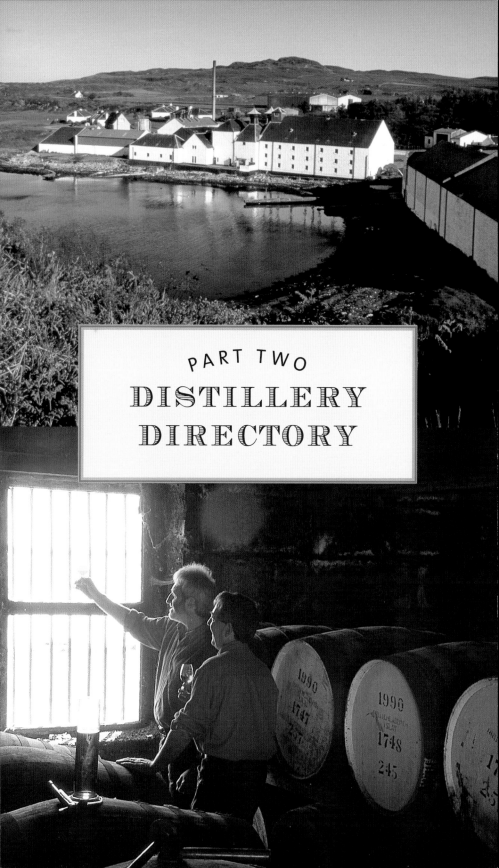

PART TWO

DISTILLERY DIRECTORY

MAP OF DISTILLERIES

Distilleries
Speyside (map below)
10–56
Isle of Jura (inset map)
73–80

1 Highland Park
2 Scapa
3 Old Pulteney
4 Clynelish
5 Glenmorangie
6 Balblair
7 Teaninich
8 Dalmore
9 Glen Ord
10 Glen Moray
11 Miltonduff
12 Glenlossie
13 Mannochmore
14 Linkwood
15 Longmorn
16 Benriach
17 Glen Elgin
18 Speyburn
19 Glen Grant
20 Glenrothes
21 Glen Spey
22 Macallan
23 Cardhu
24 Tamdhu
25 Knockando
26 Craigallechie
27 Balvenie

28 Glenfiddich
29 Glendullan
30 Mortlach
31 Dufftown
32 Aberlour
33 Glenallachie
34 Benrinnes
35 Glenfarclas
36 Tormore
37 Cragganmore
38 Dailuaine
39 Glenlivet
40 Tamnavulin
41 Tomintoul
42 Balmenach
43 Speyside
44 Tomatin
45 Royal Brackla
46 Inchgower
47 Macduff (Glen
   Deveron)
48 Aultmore
49 Strathisla
50 Strathmill
51 Glen Keith
52 Knockdhu (An
   Cnoc)
53 Glendronach
54 Ardmore
55 Auchroisk
56 Benromach
57 Glen Garioch
58 Royal Lochnagar

59 Old Fettercairn
60 Blair Athol
61 Edradour
62 Aberfeldy
63 Glenturret
64 Tullibardine
65 Deanston
66 Glengoyne
67 Loch Lomond
68 Oban
69 Ben Nevis
70 Dalwhinnie
71 Tobermory
72 Talisker

73 Bunnahabhain
74 Bruichladdich
75 Bowmore
76 Caol Ila
77 Isle of Jura
78 Laphroig
79 Lagavulin
80 Ardbeg
81 Glen Scotia
82 Springbank
83 Isle of Arran
84 Auchentoshan
85 Glenkinchie
86 Bladnoch

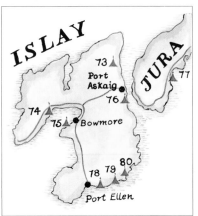

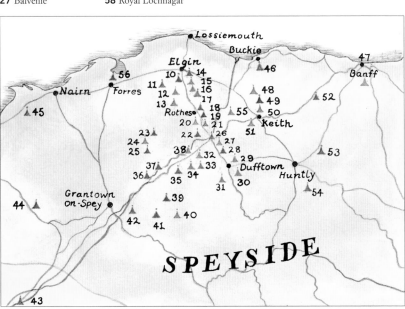

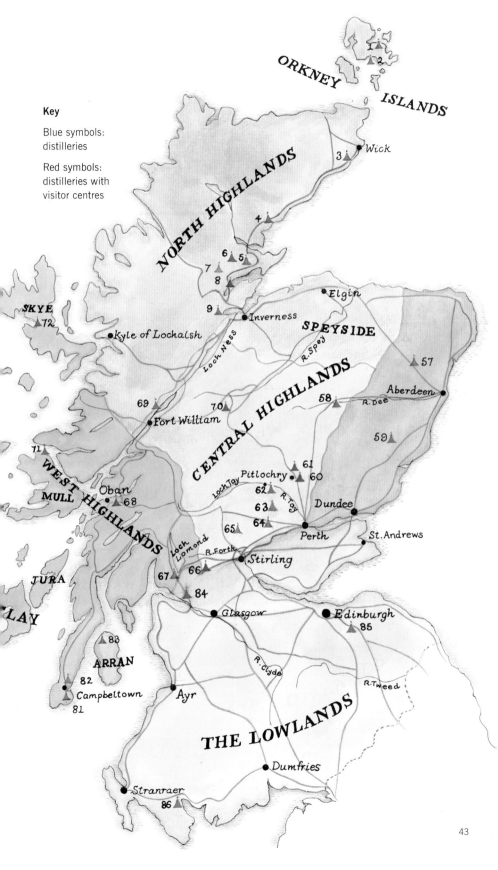

Blue symbols:
distilleries

Red symbols:
distilleries with
visitor centres

ORKNEY
ISLANDS

1
2

NORTH HIGHLANDS

3 ▲ Wick

4

6 5
7
8

9 • Elgin

• Inverness

SKYE
72

• Kyle of Lochalsh

Loch Ness

SPEYSIDE

R. Spey

57

CENTRAL HIGHLANDS

Aberdeen

58 R. Dee

69
70

59

Fort William

71

WEST HIGHLANDS

61
Pitlochry 60

Loch Tay

62 R. Tay

63

Dundee

64

MULL

Oban
68

65

Perth

St. Andrews

JURA

Loch
Lomond

R. Forth

Stirling

67 66

84

ISLAY

• Glasgow

• Edinburgh
85

83

R. Clyde

ARRAN

R. Tweed

82
Campbeltown
81

Ayr

THE LOWLANDS

86 Stranraer

• Dumfries

ABERFELDY

{*aber*-FELL-*dee*}

The site of Aberfeldy distillery was chosen for its proximity to a good water supply and the Victorian railway line to Perth. It was built in 1896 by Tommy Dewar, the younger son of John Dewar who founded Dewar & Sons of Perth. Beside the distillery is an original 1939 Barclays steam locomotive – the *Dailuaine No. 1* – that delivered coal and grain and left loaded with casks of matured whisky. The label on the bottle features the founder, John Dewer, and the distillery as it was in the nineteenth century.

Aberfeldy's original late-Victorian buildings are spoiled somewhat by a 1970s still-house extension. However, the original floor maltings have been sensitively converted to a fine visitor centre, "Dewar's World of Whisky", which recounts the history of the Dewar family, company and world-famous White Label blends.

The water source is Pitilie Burn, which flows from springs that originally supplied Pitilie distillery in the mid-nineteenth century. Scottish barley is now malted to order and dried using a moderate amount of peat. The distillery operates a computer-controlled stainless steel mash tun, 8 Siberian larch washbacks, and 4 large, bulbous pot stills. The wash is fermented for about 48 hours, using a mix of distillery and brewers' yeast, and carbon dioxide is extracted from the washbacks by fans. The whisky is matured in Spanish and American oak casks.

Aberfeldy malt whisky is available at 12 years old, as featured, a special 1980 vintage cask strength, and as a 25 years old edition. It is the signature malt in Dewar's White Label blend, which has been America's best-selling Scotch whisky for over a century. Other bottlings of Aberfeldy malt whisky are available from Adelphi and Gordon & MacPhail.

The "World of Whisky" visitor centre is excellent. It follows the story of the House of Dewar, started by John Dewar with a modest wine and spirit shop in Perth in 1846, and built by his sons and successors into an international company now selling in over 200 countries. There is a triple screen audio-visual presentation in a comfortable auditorium and personal audio handsets, with a commentary in five languages. There is also a fine exhibition with various interactive games and challenges to test the visitor's knowledge of whisky.

A guided tour of Aberfeldy distillery is included in the admission price, and exclusive bottles, gifts and souvenirs can be purchased in the Brand Store. The visitor centre is open all year and offers light refreshments, as well as a free dram of Dewar's White Label. There is a nature trail beside the burn where lucky visitors may spot one of the rare red squirrels, and there are many places of interest in and around Aberfeldy.

Feature	Profile
●●	Body
●●	Sweetness
●●	Smoky
	Medicinal
	Tobacco
●●	Honey
●	Spicy
●●	Winey
●●	Nutty
●●	Malty
●●	Fruity
●●	Floral

Age 12 years
Strength 40%
Nose Fragrant, citric zest aroma, with light smoke, honey and spice discernible
Taste Fresh, fruity and malty, medium-sweet with floral, oak and honey notes
Cluster B Medium-bodied, medium-sweet, with nutty, malty, floral, honey and fruity notes
Similar to Blair Athol, Benromach, Scapa

ABERLOUR

{*aber*-LOW-*er*}

Aberlour distillery is located in the heart of Aberlour village, on the banks of the Lour Burn where it meets the River Spey. The name Aberlour is Gaelic for the "mouth of the chattering burn". It was founded in 1879 by the philanthropist James Fleming, whose motto "Let The Deed Show" appears on every bottle. It was largely rebuilt following a fire in 1898, which started in the malt mill and destroyed most of the distillery. Further improvements were made in the 1920s, after World War II, in the 1960s, and in the 1970s.

Exceptionally soft water is drawn from several springs in the Lour Glen, which have flowed through peat, over the hard granite hills surrounding Ben Rinnes. The distillery is oil-fired, and uses a stainless steel mash tun, a stainless steel washback, and 4 copper pot stills. The malt is supplied to order and is lightly peated. Aberlour malt whiskies have benefited from greater use of oloroso sherry casks in recent years which, combined with bourbon casks, add to the whisky's complexity.

The 10 years old (profiled) has been awarded the International Wine and Spirit Competition's Gold Medal on several occasions. Aberlour also produces a 15 years old Sherry Wood finish, a 30 years old, special bottlings such as Aberlour Antique, a cask-strength version not chill-filtered and Aberlour a'bunadh Silver Label.

Aberlour distillery has a visitor centre which is reserved for trade visitors at present. Tours are not currently available, but it does have an informative website, an on-line shop, and a newsletter available by e-mail.

Feature	Profile
●●●	Body
●●●	Sweetness
●	Smoky
	Medicinal
	Tobacco
●●●●	Honey
●●●	Spicy
●●	Winey
●●	Nutty
●●●	Malty
●●●	Fruity
●●	Floral

Age 10 years
Strength 40%
Nose Spicy, estery and sherried, showing pear-drops, pine and mint-toffee
Taste Medium-bodied, medium-sweet and multi-layered. Honey evident with spice, fruit and malty toffee notes, and a whiff of smoke in the finish
Cluster B Medium-bodied, medium-sweet, with nutty, malty, floral, honey and fruity notes
Similar to Strathisla, Benrinnes

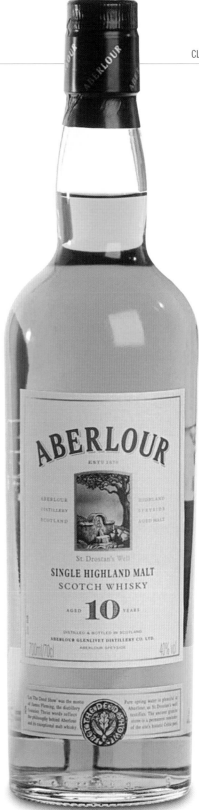

47

AN CNOC

{*an*-KNOCK}

Knockdhu distillery was founded in 1894 by John Morrison, following the discovery of several springs of purest, crystal clear water on the southern slopes of Knock Hill. The location was perfect, being within a few miles of the fertile farmlands of Moray, a district noted for its barley, and on the edge of an inexhaustible supply of peat, essential ingredients in the making of an excellent malt whisky. The surrounding crofting community also offered an ideal source of labour, and for transport of supplies and whisky it was connected to the Great Highland railway line with its own station and siding.

The distillery is attractively constructed using local grey granite. Its malt mill was replaced in 1928 as the original exploded, on one occasion partly demolishing the still house, raising the roof and setting fire to the rafters. During World War II Knockdhu housed a unit of the Indian Army, with stables and a slaughterhouse being constructed for the preparation of the soldiers' food.

After another closure, the distillery was reopened in 1989 and now produces excellent malt whiskies from its two original pot stills. During recent renovations a message from John Smith of Huntly, who built the distillery in 1894, was found in a bottle under the plaster. It was replaced by a new time capsule, sealed in an empty bottle of An Cnoc, and buried in the stillhouse wall in 2001. The main brand is called "An Cnoc", which is Gaelic for "black hill" and is so named because of the natural spring water it draws from three springs on Knock Hill. It operates a traditional cast iron mash tun, 6 Oregon pine washbacks and 2 squat stills incorporating boil balls in the neck to increase reflux. The profiled malt is An Cnoc 12 years old Single Highland Malt

Scotch Whisky. There is also a limited edition, unfiltered Knockdhu 23 years old bottled at 57.5%, and other vintages are available through independents.

An Cnoc does not have a visitor centre, but visitors are welcome by appointment.

Feature	Profile
●	Body
●●●	Sweetness
●●	Smoky
	Medicinal
	Tobacco
●●	Honey
	Spicy
	Winey
●●	Nutty
●●	Malty
●●●	Fruity
●●	Floral

Age 12 years
Strength 40%
Nose Lemon, honey and fruit aromas, with a hint of herbs
Taste Sweet and fairly complex with lots of fruit and nutty, creamy notes, and a whiff of smoke
Cluster D Light, medium-sweet, low or no peat, with fruity, floral, malty notes and nutty hints
Similar to Cardhu, Tamdhu, Aultmore

ARDBEG

{*ard*-BEG}

Ardbeg distillery was founded in 1815 by John MacDougall, on a site that had been a favourite landing spot for smugglers throughout the eighteenth century. It is in a remote, windswept cove on the south-east shore of Islay and is approached by a narrow road weaving through beautiful, rugged countryside. The sense of mystery and intrigue is heightened by nearby Kildalton Cross, a sixth-century Celtic relic from Ardbeg's historic past.

A most atmospheric distillery, where the old kiln and malt barn have recently been converted into a fine visitor centre and where a friendly welcome awaits. In 1998 Ardbeg was voted "Distillery of the Year" by the magazine *Malt Advocate*.

Ardbeg distillery is a definite "must" for visitors to Islay. As well as touring the distillery and sampling the whiskies, visitors can have a light lunch or afternoon tea in the old kiln restaurant. There is an ancient "Boby mill" for grinding the malted barley into a grist, an unusual spirit still and a museum which tells the story of Ardbeg's past.

For those not able to visit Ardbeg in person, virtual tours of the distillery are available at the website. There is also an Ardbeg Committee where members hold virtual Extraordinary Committee Meetings – accompanied by a dram of Ardbeg, naturally.

Ardbeg's beautifully soft water flows from nearby Loch Uigeadail through rocks and peat mosses to the distillery. It operates a stainless steel semi-Lauter mash tun, encased in the original cast iron tun, 6 Oregon pine washbacks and 2 large stills. The spirit still has a purifier in the neck. The whisky is matured in American oak bourbon first fill and refill casks. The single 10 years old malt (profiled below) is the most phenolic of all the Islay whiskies, with peat and smoke to the fore, balanced by malt and spice flavours and more than a hint of salty Atlantic air. In addition to the 10 years old, which is not chill-filtered, Ardbeg also offers a 17 years old, a 1977 vintage and a "Lord of the Isles" 25 years old edition.

Feature	Profile
●●●●	Body
●	Sweetness
●●●●	Smoky
●●●●	Medicinal
	Tobacco
	Honey
●●	Spicy
	Winey
●	Nutty
●●	Malty
●	Fruity
	Floral

Age 10 years
Strength 46%
Nose Peaty, salty and malty with hints of bourbon and tangy orange
Taste Smoke and iodine evident with spice, cocoa and liquorice notes also showing
Cluster J Full-bodied, dry, pungent, peaty and medicinal, with spicy, tobacco notes
Similar to Talisker, Clynelish, Lagavulin

ARDMORE

*{ard-*MORE}

Ardmore distillery was built in 1898 by Adam Teacher for William Teacher & Sons. It is situated beside the River Bogie, in rolling countryside famed for its barley and Aberdeen Angus beef. Nearby is Leith Hall (see above), a picturesque seventeenth-century Scottish baronial mansion house with witches' hats for turrets and attractively themed gardens.

It is a large distillery, extended in 1955 and 1974, and is home to the principal malt of the Teacher's blends. The water is drawn from springs that rise in Knockandy Hill and its malted barley, supplied to order, is probably the most peated on Speyside. The distillery operates an interesting Boby mill, a fine copper-topped mash tun, 14 Oregon pine washbacks, 4 wash and 4 spirit pot stills. Three yeasts are used in the fermentation, which typically lasts 54 hours. The stills were converted from coal-fired to steam heating in 2001, increasing production capacity to around 70,000 litres (1.3 million pints) of spirit per week.

The whisky is matured at the distillery in American oak bourbon and refill casks. Most of Ardmore's production is used for blending in Teacher's Highland Cream. Ardmore 12 years old Single Highland Malt (profiled) was bottled in 1999 for the distillery's Centenary. It is difficult to find, as it is a rather expensive 21 years old vintage. Other vintages are available from Gordon & MacPhail and Cadenhead's.

Ardmore distillery has no visitor centre and does not offer tours. However, Ardmore single malts can be purchased at its sister distillery, Glendronach. Failing that, Teacher's Highland Cream is a blend that contains a high proportion of malt whiskies, with Ardmore well to the fore.

Feature	Profile
●●	Body
●●	Sweetness
●●	Smoky
	Medicinal
	Tobacco
●	Honey
●	Spicy
●	Winey
●●	Nutty
●●●	Malty
●	Fruity
●	Floral

Age 12 years
Strength 40%
Nose Medium sweet, creamy and smoky
Taste Mellow and malty, with balanced sweetness and buttery, oaky and peaty notes
Cluster F Medium-bodied, medium-sweet, low peat, malty notes and sherry, honey, spicy hints
Similar to Deanston, Old Fettercairn, Tomatin

ISLE OF ARRAN

{Arr-en}

Isle of Arran is Scotland's newest distillery, founded in 1995 at Lochranza village on the north of Arran, one of the most beautiful locations in Scotland. Despite the recent date of its only licensed distillery, Arran has a long history of whisky-making. In the nineteenth century it is estimated that there were more than 50 whisky producers on Arran, most of which were illegal. It is not surprising, therefore, that the term "Arran Water" is synonymous with whisky, and at one time the whisky produced here was said to be the best in Scotland. However, the island's remoteness and the cost of transportation forced the producers to close.

It took the inspirational leadership of the distillery's founder Harold Curry, formerly of Chivas Bros and House of Campbell, to resurrect the whisky industry on Arran. The Isle of Arran distillery is of a modern, purpose-built design that cleverly incorporates a pagoda-chimney on the roof of its visitor centre and production buildings.

The distillery draws soft, peaty water from Loch na Davie and operates a stainless steel mash tun, 4 Oregon pine washbacks and 2 specially-designed copper stills. The whisky is matured in a mixture of American white oak bourbon casks, and refill and fresh sherry European oak casks. The atmosphere of sea breezes and clear mountain air helps mature the Arran malt to perfection and adds a seashore dimension to the flavour.

Isle of Arran single malt is available at 5 years old (profiled) and as a more heavily sherried 5 years old special edition. The distillery also offers 2 blended whiskies, Loch Ranza, in a distinctive blue bottle, and Robert Burns. There is also a Holy Isle Cream Liqueur that combines the whisky with cream.

The visitor centre was officially opened in 1997 by HM The Queen during her final voyage on the Royal Yacht Britannia. It is open all year and offers guided tours, an audio-visual presentation, an exhibition and tastings. The exhibition includes a replica of an eighteenth-century Crofters' Inn, a smugglers' tunnel and a spectacular waterfall. It has been highly commended by the Scottish Tourist Board.

Feature	Profile
●●	Body
●●●	Sweetness
●	Smoky
●	Medicinal
	Tobacco
●	Honey
●	Spicy
●	Winey
	Nutty
●	Malty
●	Fruity
●●	Floral

Age 5 years
Strength 43%
Nose Aromatic and estery, with a sherry note and a whiff of salt and smoke
Taste Sweet and floral, malt and honey notes and some fruit and sherry
Cluster G Medium-bodied, sweet, low peat and floral notes
Similar to Speyburn, Glen Spey, Dufftown

AUCHENTOSHAN

{OCH-*en*-TOSH-*an*}

Auchentoshan is Gaelic for "corner of the field". The distillery was first licensed in 1823 and is located in Dalmuir at the foot of the Kilpatrick hills. From its position on the Clyde, it has seen the evolution of shipping, from schooners such as the Cutty Sark to the Queen Elizabeth II on her maiden voyage. It was rebuilt in 1875, bombed in World War II, repaired in 1949, re-equipped in 1974, and refurbished in the late 1980s.

Auchentoshan is one of three distilleries classified as Lowland along with Bladnoch and Glenkinchie. It is the last Lowland distillery to employ triple distillation, whereby the output from the wash still is distilled twice more to produce a lighter, more refined spirit. Its whisky has thereby earned the title of "The Lowland Malt".

The distillery's process water is supplied from Loch Katrine and its cooling water is collected in a World War II bomb crater in the hills. It uses unpeated malt, supplied to order, and operates a copper-topped stainless steel mash tun, 4 Oregon pine washbacks, and 3 stills. The spirit emerges from the wash still at 18% alcohol, at 54% from the intermediate still, and at 81% from the spirit still – the highest strength of any Scotch whisky. It is matured in a mixture of American bourbon and Spanish sherry casks, including some oloroso and Pedro Jimenez casks, specially prepared in Spain.

Auchentoshan Lowland Single Malt whisky is available at 10 years old (profiled), and as Auchentoshan Select, which has no age statement. Other bottlings are at 21, 22, 25 and 31 years old. There is also a "Three Wood" edition with no age statement, matured in American bourbon hogsheads, oloroso sherry and Pedro Jimenez Sherry butts, and a cask strength 18 years old vintage 1978. The malts have won several international gold medals.

Tours are available by appointment and the distillery hopes to open a visitor centre soon.

Feature	Profile
	Body
●●	Sweetness
	Smoky
	Medicinal
	Tobacco
●	Honey
●	Spicy
	Winey
●●	Nutty
●●	Malty
●●●	Fruity
●●●	Floral

Age 10 years
Strength 40%
Nose Fragrant, fresh and bursting with lemon zest
Taste Fruity citrus and raisins, muesli and satsumas, with a dusting of cinnamon
Cluster D Light, medium-sweet, low or no peat, with fruity, floral, malty notes and nutty hints
Similar to Glengoyne, Cardhu, Aultmore

AUCHROISK

{*oth*-RUSK}

Auchroisk distillery was built in 1974 as a model distillery, with a showcase still-house containing eight lantern-headed pot stills arranged in two neat rows. Auchroisk is Gaelic for "ford across the red stream". It was felt that the name would be too difficult for customers to use so the malt it produces was called "The Singleton". A Victorian steam engine from Strathmill distillery is preserved as a showpiece in the entrance hall.

Auchroisk draws its water from Dorie's well which is very soft, of exceptional quality, and the reason for the distillery's location. It operates a stainless steel mash tun, 8 stainless steel washbacks and 8 stills. The whisky is matured in American oak bourbon casks. However, it was among the first in the industry to apply a sherry finish to its malt whisky, which is finished in sherry casks for the final year.

Auchroisk Single Speyside Malt whisky (profiled) is available at 10 years old in Guinness UDV's Flora and Fauna series. It was also bottled under the previous management of Justerini and Brooks at 10 years old, at 12 years old cask strength (59.3%), and in occasional vintage editions. It is also available as Auchroisk through independent bottlers, but generally without any sherry wood finish. The bulk of the production goes for blending, and it is used principally in Guinness UDV's J&B blend. The Singleton is a highly regarded "designer" malt whisky that has won several awards in international competitions. The emblem of Auchroisk is the swift, which raise their young under the eaves of the distillery buildings.

Auchroisk distillery does not have a visitor centre or offer tours.

Feature	Profile
●●	Body
●●●	Sweetness
●	Smoky
	Medicinal
	Tobacco
●●	Honey
●	Spicy
●●	Winey
●●	Nutty
●●	Malty
●●	Fruity
●	Floral

Age 10 years
Strength 43%
Nose Fragrant and honeyed with a whiff of smoke
Taste Medium-bodied, with a pronounced sherry note, nuts, autumn berries, and vanilla
Cluster F Medium-bodied, medium-sweet, low peat, malty notes and sherry, honey, spicy hints
Similar to Glenrothes, Glen Keith, Deanston

SPEYSIDE
SINGLE MALT
SCOTCH WHISKY

In a striking *hilltop location, visible from ROTHES,* is sited the

AUCHROISK

distillery. The unusual name, *meaning "FORD of the RED STREAM" in Gaelic,* refers to the MULBEN BURN *from which the distillery draws its cooling water.* However, *the principal reason for the siting of the distillery is DORIES WELL an abundant source of soft, pure springwater.* Through *the smoke and nutty sweetness, comes the unmistakeable feel of DORIES silky water, followed by a dry, well balanced finish.*

AGED **10** YEARS

45% vol   Distilled & Bottled in SCOTLAND AUCHROISK DISTILLERY, Mulben, Keith, Banffshire, Scotland   70cl

AULTMORE

{*olt*-MORE}

The Aultmore distillery was built in 1896 by Alexander Edward near Keith, and rebuilt in 1971 above the river Isla, with a doubled capacity and rather functional buildings. Aultmore is Gaelic for "the big burn" and the distillery's emblem of a dipper, an aquatic songbird which can sometimes be seen in the Forgie Burn behind the distillery.

Water is drawn from Auchinderran Burn, and the distillery operates a stainless steel Lauter mash tun, 6 Siberian larch washbacks and 4 stills.

The whisky is matured in American bourbon casks.

Aultmore Single Highland Malt whisky is available at 12 years old (profiled) in Guinness UDV's Flora and Fauna range and in Signatory Gordon & MacPhail's Connoisseurs' edition. A new edition is due to become available by late-2002. It is used in Dewar's blends, which currently account for the bulk of its production.

Aultmore distillery welcomes visitors by appointment.

Feature	Profile
●●	Body
●●	Sweetness
●	Smoky
	Medicinal
	Tobacco
●	Honey
	Spicy
	Winey
●●	Nutty
●●	Malty
●●	Fruity
●●	Floral

Age 12 years
Strength 43%
Nose Aromatic and fragrant with a whiff of smoke
Taste Fruit and floral, buttery with a hint of honey and peat
Cluster D Light, medium-sweet, low or no peat, with fruity, floral, malty notes and nutty hints
Similar to Speyside, Cardhu, Tobermory

SIGNATORY VINTAGE
SCOTCH WHISKY CO. LTD.

Vintage 1986
Single Highland Malt Scotch Whisky

Matured in an oak cask for 14 years
Distilled at Aultmore Distillery

on 21.5.86 *Bottled 11.9.2000*

Cask No. 1958 Bottle No. **223** *of 108*

*This whisky has been selected, produced and bottled in
Scotland for and under the sole responsibility of
Signatory Vintage Scotch Whisky Co. Ltd
Edinburgh EH6 5PY Scotland*

70cl 43%vol
NATURAL COLOUR

BALBLAIR

{*bal*-BLAIR}

Founded in 1790 by John Ross, Balblair distillery is the industry's second oldest working distillery. It is situated in a beautiful part of the country, where the Allt Dearg Burns flow down the Struie Hill to the farmlands of Edderton (known as the "parish of the peats") on the shore of the Dornoch Firth. The distillery was rebuilt on a new site in 1894 and extended to 3 steam-heated stills in the 1960s. Its original riveted wash still is the only one of its type left in the industry. All its warehouses are earth-floored, except one that was converted by the army in World War II for use as a canteen.

The air in Edderton on the Dornoch Firth, where Balblair is distilled, is considered to be the purest in Scotland. It has been swept across the vast expanse of the North Sea by Arctic winds, giving it a sharp clean edge; it has swirled around Cambuscurrie Bay, picking up a hint of saltiness; and has rushed through bristling coastal pine woods which imbue it with freshness. It is this pure air that is said to give Balblair whisky its smooth, light, delicate and refreshing taste.

In addition to the featured 16 years old Balblair Single Highland Malt Scotch Whisky, there is an unaged version Balblair Elements, and a 31 years old Highland Selection bottled at cask strength (45%).

Balblair is one of the most attractive small distilleries and has remained largely unchanged since the nineteenth century. There is no visitor centre, but visitors are welcome by appointment.

Feature	Profile
●●	Body
●●●	Sweetness
●●	Smoky
●	Medicinal
	Tobacco
	Honey
●●	Spicy
	Winey
●●	Nutty
●	Malty
●●	Fruity
●	Floral

Age 16 years
Strength 40%
Nose Fresh with a smoky note and a touch of the sea
Taste Medium-sweet, with citrus fruits, and spicy, nutty and smoky notes
Cluster H Medium-bodied, medium-sweet, with smoky, fruity, spicy notes and floral, nutty hints
Similar to Craigellachie, Oban, Glenmorangie

BALBLAIR

SINGLE MALT SCOTCH WHISKY

Distilled Where
the Air is said to be
The Purest in Scotland

Aged **16** Years

70cl℮ 40%vol
INVER HOUSE DISTILLERS LTD
ML6 8PL SCOTLAND

BALMENACH

*{bal-*MEN*-ach}*

almenach distillery was one of the earliest to be licensed by James McGregor in 1824, at a time when illicit distilling was a way of life. Situated above the village of Cromdale, one of the crossing points of the River Spey, the distillery stands on historic soil. On the nearby hill of Tom Lethendry are the ruins of an old castle where, in 1690, the defeated Jacobites took refuge after the battle of the Haughs of Cromdale. The distillery was reconstructed in 1920,

extended to 6 stills in 1962 and had its mash-house rebuilt in 1968. After a period of inactivity, it was acquired by Inver House Distillers in 1997 and has been restored to full working order.

Its water is drawn from Rasmudin Burn, and the distillery operates a traditional copper-domed cast iron mash tun, 6 Oregon pine washbacks and 6 squat stills incorporating boil balls in their necks to increase reflux. The whisky is matured in a mixture of

American bourbon, European sherry and refill casks, in dunnage warehouses.

Balmenach Single Highland Malt whisky is available at 12 years old (profiled) in Guinness UDV's Flora and Fauna range, and in the Rare Malts series at 22 years old (60.1%). Inver House Distillers produce special versions, such as 27 years old "Highland Selection" (46%), and Balmenach whiskies are also available through independents. We look forward to the new, less peated whisky in about 2009. The distillery has no visitor centre, but visitors are welcome.

Feature	Profile
●●●●	Body
●●●	Sweetness
●●	Smoky
	Medicinal
	Tobacco
●●	Honey
●	Spicy
●●●	Winey
●●●	Nutty
	Malty
●	Fruity
●●	Floral

Age 12 years
Strength 43%
Nose Aromatic, floral and nutty with a sherried nose and a whiff of smoke
Taste Full bodied, medium sweet, with vanilla, honey and sherry notes, and a spicy finish
Cluster A Full-bodied, medium-sweet, pronounced sherry with fruity, spicy, malty notes and nutty, smoky hints
Similar to Mortlach, Dailuaine, Macallan

BALVENIE

{*bal*-VENN-*ee*}

Balvenie distillery takes its name from nearby Balvenie Castle and was founded in 1892 by William Grant, who also built the Glenfiddich distillery next door. Some of the barley used by the distillery is grown on its own farm, and it is one of the few to have retained traditional floor maltings, where the germinating grain is turned by hand three times a day using traditional wooden shiels.

It is an attractive Victorian distillery whose buildings have remained largely unchanged for a century. The maltings boast a single pagoda vent, and the kilns are still fired by coal and peat. The distillery operates a stainless steel mash tun, 10 Douglas fir washbacks, 5 wash stills and 8 spirit stills. Its water is drawn from Robbie Dubh Burn, the source shared with Glenfiddich, but their whiskies are quite different. This is due to the different types of cask used

for maturation – Balvenie uses more European sherry oak casks. Balvenie also has its own coopers to maintain the casks, and a coppersmith to tend the stills.

Balvenie distillery produces Founder's Reserve 10 years old (profiled), Balvenie DoubleWood 12 years old and Balvenie Single Barrel at 15 and 25 years old. DoubleWood is first matured in a traditional whisky cask and then finished in an original sherry oak cask – it consequently offers more sherry complexity than Founder's Reserve. Balvenie Single Barrel is a vintage whisky from a single cask, matured at least 15 years and bottled at 50%. Also available as rare malts Balvenie PortWood, aged 21 years, and Balvenie Vintage Cask, aged over 30 years.

The distillery does not have a visitor centre, but the full range of its whiskies can be purchased from Glenfiddich.

Feature	Profile
●●●	Body
●●	Sweetness
●	Smoky
	Medicinal
	Tobacco
●●●	Honey
●●	Spicy
●	Winey
	Nutty
●●	Malty
●●	Fruity
●●	Floral

Age 10 years
Strength 40%
Nose Sweet and smoky, with a hint of sherry
Taste Honey, spice, and all things nice – flowers, fruit, malt and a long finish. Robust and medium-sweet
Cluster C Medium-bodied, medium-sweet, with fruity, floral, honey, malty notes and spicy hints
Similar to Benriach, Glen Ord, Glendullan

EST? 1892

SINGLE MALT

Distilled at

THE BALVENIE®

Distillery Banffshire

SCOTLAND

FOUNDER'S RESERVE
MALT SCOTCH WHISKY

AGED **10** YEARS

The Balvenie Distillery has been owned
AND MANAGED BY OUR INDEPENDENT
family company for five generations.

AT BALVENIE

there are four maltmen, three mashmen
three tun room men, and three stillmen
AND BETWEEN THEM
they make all The Balvenie we bottle

THE BALVENIE MALTMASTER

THE BALVENIE DISTILLERY COMPANY, BALVENIE MALTINGS, DUFFTOWN,
BANFFSHIRE, SCOTLAND AB55 4BB
PRODUCT OF SCOTLAND

70cle   40%vol

BEN NEVIS

{*ben*-NEV-*is*}

Ben Nevis distillery was built in 1825 by John Macdonald, a farmer from Wester Ross, and his whisky was sold as "Long John's Dew of Ben Nevis". The name stuck and was later used for a blend called "Long John", which is sadly no longer available. Queen Victoria visited the distillery during her tour of Scotland in 1848, and the distillery subsequently sent a barrel of whisky to Buckingham Palace for the Prince of Wales's 21st birthday.

The distillery was rebuilt in 1865, and there were further modifications in 1887, when a pier was added on Loch Linnhe, and in 1894 when it was connected to the West Highland Railway. A Coffey still was introduced in 1955 to produce grain whisky, thereby enabling Ben Nevis distillery to make blended whisky.

Its water is drawn from Allt a Mhullin "the Mill Stream" which flows from two small lochs on the north face of Ben Nevis, Britain's highest mountain. The distillery operates a large stainless steel mash tun, 6 stainless steel washbacks and 4 swan-necked pot stills – producing around 750,000 litres (1.3 million pints) a year. The whisky is matured in 7 warehouses at the distillery, using ex-bourbon American oak and ex-sherry European oak casks.

Ben Nevis Single Highland Malt whisky is available at 10 years old (profiled), an 8 years old vatted malt "Glencoe" (58%), a 15 years old sherry finish and a cask-strength 26 years old (52%). It is also used in the company's Special Reserve blend, and a 12 years old de luxe blend. The 10 years old malt won a Grand Gold Medal at the Mondé Selection de la Qualité, Belgium in 1999 and 2000, and a further Gold Medal in 2001.

The distillery's visitor centre in a former warehouse dating from 1862, offers tours, tastings, a "Legend of the Dew of Ben Nevis" audio-visual presentation, an exhibition, a coffee shop and restaurant.

Feature	Profile
●●●●	Body
●●	Sweetness
●●	Smoky
	Medicinal
	Tobacco
●●	Honey
●●	Spicy
	Winey
●●	Nutty
●●	Malty
●●	Fruity
●●	Floral

Age 10 years
Strength 46%
Nose Aromatic and estery, with some spice and smoke evident
Taste Creamy caramels, fruit and oak, with a peaty finish – a very well-balanced profile
Cluster B Medium-bodied, medium-sweet, with nutty, malty, floral, honey and fruity notes
Similar to Benromach, Benrinnes

BEN NEVIS

Ten Years Old
DISTILLED AND BOTTLED IN SCOTLAND

SINGLE HIGHLAND MALT
SCOTCH WHISKY
BEN NEVIS DISTILLERY (FORT WILLIAM) LIMITED

70cl   46% vol

BENRIACH

{ben-REE-ach}

Benriach distillery has had a chequered history. Named after Riach Farm nearby, it was built in 1898 by John Duff who also built its sister distillery Longmorn. The location was chosen for its proximity to the Great North of Scotland Railway, to which it was connected by a siding from Longmorn Station.

However, the distillery closed soon after completion in 1900 and lay dormant for over 60 years. Happily, it was restarted in 1965 and extended in 1985. It is a delightful, Victorian stone distillery with a pagoda chimney which is a landmark in the Glen of Rothes. The emblem on the Benriach bottle is a wild red stag, and these can sometimes be heard roaring in the nearby Teindland Forest.

The distillery draws its water from Burnside Spring, and uses lightly peated malted barley. It operates a stainless steel mash tun, 4 steel washbacks and 4 small pot stills. The whisky is matured in a mixture of American bourbon casks, European sherry casks, and refills. Production is high at 3.5 million litres (6 million pints) a year, most of which goes for blending. Benriach Single Highland Malt is available at 10 years old (profiled), and occasionally through independents. It is also used in Chivas Regal and other Chivas blends.

Benriach distillery does not have a visitor centre or offer tours.

Loading barrels onto a "Puggy" at the siding of Benriach distillery.
The Puggy was used until the mid 1980s.

Feature	Profile
●●	Body
●●	Sweetness
●	Smoky
	Medicinal
	Tobacco
●●	Honey
●●	Spicy
	Winey
	Nutty
●●	Malty
●●●	Fruity
●●	Floral

Age 10 years
Strength 43%
Nose Light, fruity and estery
Taste Flowery and fruity, with malty caramel notes and a hint of smoke
Cluster C Medium-bodied, medium-sweet, with fruity, floral, honey, malty notes and spicy hints
Similar to Dalwhinnie, Balvenie, Glen Ord

BENRIACH DISTILLERY
EST. 1898
A SINGLE
PURE HIGHLAND MALT
Scotch Whisky
Benriach Distillery, in the heart of the Highlands, still malts its own barley. The resulting whisky has a unique and attractive delicacy
PRODUCED AND BOTTLED BY THE
BENRIACH
DISTILLERY C°
ELGIN, MORAYSHIRE, SCOTLAND, IV30 3SJ
Distilled and Bottled in Scotland
AGED 10 YEARS
70 cl ℮ 43% vol

BENRINNES

*{ben-*RIN-*is}*

Lying high on Ben Rinnes, whose 840 metre (2,800 feet) summit dominates Speyside and the Moray Firth, is the rather remote and functional Benrinnes distillery. Because of its height, supplies were originally brought by horse and cart from Aberlour station, three miles away. The emblem on the bottle is the blackcock, or male grouse, a local resident of the surrounding moors.

In 1826, Peter McKenzie of Whitehouse Farm was recorded as the licensed distiller. The distillery moved to its present site in 1829 following a flood, and by 1842 it existed as a farm whose outbuildings were used for distillation. Benrinnes was still a working farm a century later, with distillery visitors and traffic being frequently delayed by the twice-daily procession of cattle for milking. Occasionally the cows took fright, at which the distillery workers would down tools and round them up.

The farming element was removed in the mid-1950s when the Benrinnes

distillery was rebuilt and, in 1966, a Saladin malting was added and the still house was extended to 6 stills. The stills are grouped in threes because some of the spirit is triple-distilled, the output from the wash still being split between an intermediate and a spirit still. Another unusual feature is the use of traditional worm tubs to condense the spirit vapours, rather than the more modern condenser method.

Water is drawn from springs that rise on Ben Rinnes, passing through granite, over peat and moss, and finally being filtered on the gravel beds of the Rowantree and Scurran burns.

The whisky is matured in a combination of bourbon and sherry casks. Most goes for blending, though the 15 years old Benrinnes Single Malt (profiled) is available in Guinness UDV's Flora and Fauna range, in the Rare Malts series at 21 years old (60.4%), and from some independents.

The distillery does not have a visitor centre or offer tours.

Feature	Profile
●●●	Body
●●	Sweetness
●●	Smoky
	Medicinal
	Tobacco
●●●	Honey
●	Spicy
●	Winey
●●	Nutty
●●●	Malty
●●	Fruity
●●	Floral

Age 15 years
Strength 43%
Nose Soft, medium-dry, with a little peat and cereal
Taste Medium-sweet, smooth, slightly smoky with grassy, flowery notes
Cluster B Medium-bodied, medium-sweet, with nutty, malty, floral, honey and fruity notes
Similar to Benromach, Aberfeldy, Ben Nevis

SPEYSIDE
SINGLE MALT
SCOTCH WHISKY

BENRINNES

distillery stands on the
northern shoulder of BEN RINNES
700 feet above sea level.
Is is ideally located to exploit
the natural advantages of the
area-pure air, peat and
barley and the finest of hill water,
which rises through granite
from springs on the summit
of the mountain. The resulting
single MALT SCOTCH WHISKY,
is rounded and mellow.

AGED **15** YEARS

Distilled & Bottled in SCOTLAND
BENRINNES DISTILLERY
Aberlour, Banffshire, Scotland.

43% vol 70 cl

BENROMACH

{ben-ROM-ach}

Benromach distillery was designed in 1898 by Charles Doig, the noted Elgin architect who was responsible for several other Speyside distilleries. Its original buildings were modernized in 1966, and extended in 1974 and 1998. The distillery has had a chequered career, with several changes of ownership and dormant periods, the last closure being in 1983 when all the distillation equipment was removed. Happily, it was rescued in 1993 by Gordon & MacPhail, the Elgin whisky merchants, and production re-commenced in 1998. Benromach's whitewashed buildings and tall red brick chimney create a striking local landmark in the lush arable landscape of the Laich of Moray.

Process water is drawn from the Romach Hills and *Chariot* barley is supplied lightly-peated to order. Benromach operates a large stainless steel mash tun, 4 larch washbacks and 2 traditional steam-heated stills. The stills are shorter than most to distil a full, rich spirit, and are currently producing about 0.5 million litres a year. The malt

whiskies are matured in traditional dunnage warehouses using new Spanish sherry casks, while the whisky for use in blends is matured in American oak bourbon barrels and refill sherry casks.

Benromach Single Speyside Malt whisky is available at 15 years old (profiled), as a "Centenary" 17 years old that has been finished in sherry casks for 2 years, a new 1974 vintage, and a cask-strength (63%) 1982 vintage. It is also still available in Guinness UDV's Rare Malts series at 21 years old (63.8%). Benromach malt whiskies have won several awards in international competitions. The new malt whisky will not be released until about 2008, and will no doubt have a different flavour profile owing to the change of equipment in 1998.

A former drier house was converted in 1999 to a Malt Whisky Centre and shop, which has been graded as a 4-star attraction by the Scottish Tourist Board. It includes a fine "Heritage Room" where the story of malt whisky is told. Benromach distillery offers tours and tastings all year.

Feature	Profile
●●	Body
●●	Sweetness
●●	Smoky
	Medicinal
	Tobacco
●●	Honey
●●	Spicy
●	Winey
●●	Nutty
●●	Malty
●●	Fruity
●●	Floral

Age 15 years
Strength 40%
Nose Aromatic and floral, with a hint of sherry
Taste Fruity, herbal and malty notes with hints of peat and spice
Cluster B Medium-bodied, medium-sweet, with nutty, malty, floral, honey and fruity notes
Similar to Blair Athol, Aberfeldy, Scapa

BLADNOCH

{BLAD-*noch*}

Bladnoch distillery was built in 1817 beside the River Bladnoch, by Thomas McClelland, and was rebuilt in 1871 by his grandson. It was extended in 1966, but has suffered periods of closure, most recently in 1993. Happily, it was bought in 2000 by Ulsterman Raymond Armstrong, and is now once again in production, though limited to a fraction of its former capacity by a covenant imposed by the previous owners. The distinctive pagoda chimney, which reaches above the rest of the complex, was once used to malt the barley grown by the McClellands. It is one of only three distilleries classified as Lowland, the others being Auchentoshan and Glenkinchie.

Along the riverside walk is the ancient oak woodland of Cotland Wood, home of the broad-leaved Helleborine, a rare orchid, which is used as the Bladnoch emblem. It will be some years before the spirit currently being produced is available to buy, but in the meantime there are existing stocks from the previous owners, prior to the closure in 1993.

Water is drawn from the River Bladnoch and the distillery operates a stainless steel mash tun, 6 Oregon pine washbacks and 2 tall pot stills, which incorporate boil balls in the neck. These boil balls help to cool the vapours so that the heavier volatiles fall back as reflux, resulting in a lighter spirit. The whisky is matured in a mixture of ex-bourbon American oak and ex-sherry European oak casks in the warehouses on the site.

Bladnoch 10 years old (profiled) is available in Guiness UDV's Flora and Fauna series, and in special editions.

The visitor centre is open from April to October, and offers a short video film, tours, tastings and a shop.

Feature	Profile
●	Body
●●	Sweetness
●	Smoky
	Medicinal
	Tobacco
	Honey
●	Spicy
●	Winey
	Nutty
●●	Malty
●●	Fruity
●●●	Floral

Age 10 years
Strength 43%
Nose Aromatic and fruity, packed with flowers and citrus fruits
Taste Moderately sweet and fruity, with a cereal note, and hints of sherry and smoke
Cluster E Light, medium-sweet, low peat, with floral, malty notes and fruity, spicy, honey hints
Similar to Bunnahabhain, Glenallachie, Glenkinchie

LOWLAND
SINGLE MALT
SCOTCH WHISKY

The *Broad Leaved Helleborine*,
a rare species of *wild orchid*, can be found growing
in the *ancient oak woodland* behind the

BLADNOCH

distillery. The most southerly in *SCOTLAND*,
founded in the *early* 1800's, & the
distillery stands by the *RIVER BLADNOCH*
near *Wigtown*. It produces a *distinctive*
LOWLAND single MALT WHISKY – delicate and
fruity with a *lemony* aroma and *taste*

AGED **10** YEARS

43% vol   70cl

Distilled & Bottled in SCOTLAND
BLADNOCH DISTILLERY, Bladnoch, Wigtownshire, Scotland

BLAIR ATHOL

*{blair-*ATH-*oll}*

The attractive, ivy-clad visitor centre at Blair Athol distillery (left), and the shop and bar (right).

The Blair Athol distillery was originally founded in 1798 by John Stewart and Robert Robertson, and was called "Aldour" after Allt Dour meaning "the burn of the otter". It lies on the edge of Pitlochry, in the Vale of Athol, which has long been famous for its whisky. Legend has it that the "mellow barley bree from the cavern of Ben Vrackie warmed the hearts and strengthened the arms of the Highlanders" when they defeated the army of William III at Killiecrankie in 1689.

The distillery operates an 8 tonne stainless steel Lauter mash tun, 4 stainless steel washbacks, 4 Oregon pine washbacks and 4 copper stills. The barley is supplied, lightly malted to order, from Glen Ord maltings. Process water is drawn from the Allt Dour, which flows from a spring high on Ben Vrackie and otters, one of which features on the distillery's bottles, can occasionally be sighted in the burn. Blair Athol's malt whiskies are matured predominately in ex-bourbon American refill casks.

Blair Athol Single Malt is available at 12 years old (profiled) in Guinness UDV's Flora and Fauna range, and from some independents. It is the heart of Bell's blends, which take more than 95% of its production.

The visitor centre is very popular due to its proximity to Edinburgh and Glasgow, and is open all year. As well as a tour of the distillery, visitors can also enjoy home baking in the coffee shop and taste a range of whiskies in the attractive bar.

Feature	Profile
●●	Body
●●	Sweetness
●●	Smoky
	Medicinal
	Tobacco
●	Honey
●●	Spicy
●●	Winey
●●	Nutty
●●	Malty
●●	Fruity
●●	Floral

Age 12 years
Strength 43%
Nose Light and dry, aromatic with honey and citrus notes
Taste Strong fruity flavour, hints of sweetness and spice with a smoky finish
Cluster B Medium-bodied, medium-sweet, with nutty, malty, floral, honey and fruity notes
Similar to Aberfeldy, Benromach, Glenturret

HIGHLAND
SINGLE MALT
SCOTCH WHISKY

BLAIR ATHOL

distillery, established in 1798, stands on *peaty moorland* in the *foothills* of the *GRAMPIAN MOUNTAINS.* An ancient source of *water* for the *distillery, ALLT DOUR BURN* – *'The Burn of the Otter',* flows close by. This *single MALT SCOTCH WHISKY* has a *mellow deep toned* aroma, a *strong fruity* flavour and a *smooth* finish.

12 YEARS

43% vol   70cl

BOWMORE

{*bow*-MORE}

With its classic whitewashed buildings and black trimmed windows, Bowmore distillery settles expansively along the shore of Loch Indaal, its pagoda-topped chimneys rising grandly above the town's High street. While its frontage is unmistakably Islay, with one seashore warehouse emblazoned "BOWMORE" in large bold letters, its malts have a fine character all their own.

It is the oldest licensed distillery on Islay, founded in 1779 by farmer David Simpson, and one of the first to offer its product widely as a single malt whisky. In the 1880s and 1890s Bowmore Islay whisky was sold throughout Britain, Ireland and Canada. The focal point of the town is a round church at the top of the hill, with no corners in which the devil could hide. This is certainly a distillery rich in legends – indeed, its most popular single malt is named Bowmore Legend.

The management flirted briefly with stainless steel washbacks in the 1980s, but reverted to traditional wooden washbacks and floor maltings in the 1990s. Some of the barley is still malted by hand on a traditional malting floor and partially dried over a peat fire, the peat being first crumbled to generate more smoke. Bowmore is only medium peated, however, with about half the phenols of its neighbours round the coast at Lagavulin, Laphroaig and Ardbeg, and as such it is not typically Islay.

Its water is drawn from the river Laggan and it operates a copper-domed mash tun, 4 Oregon pine washbacks and 4 pot stills. The whisky is matured in Spanish and American oak casks, some stored in the famous Bowmore Vaults below sea level, and about a third are prepared with oloroso sherry. The warm water from the condensers is used to heat a swimming pool in a former warehouse, converted by the distillery for the use of the residents.

Bowmore Single Islay Malt whisky is available at 12 years old (profiled), and at 15, 17, 21, 25 and 30 years old. It is also offered as Bowmore Legend, a cask strength version (56%) with no age statement, and Darkest Islay, finished in oloroso sherry casks. Bowmore malt whiskies have won many international awards, including the prestigious "Distiller of the Year" in 1995, the International Spirits Challenge 2000, and the San Francisco World Spirits Competition 2000 and 2001.

Bowmore distillery has an excellent visitor centre offering an audio-visual presentation, tours and tastings. The visitor centre and a well-stocked shop are open all year.

Feature	Profile
●●	Body
●●	Sweetness
●●●	Smoky
●●	Medicinal
	Tobacco
●●	Honey
●●	Spicy
●	Winey
●	Nutty
●	Malty
●	Fruity
●●	Floral

Age 12 years
Strength 40%
Nose Grassy and smoky, with a lemon note, and hints of sherry and seaweed
Taste Well balanced complexity with smoke, spice, heather, honey and chocolate
Cluster I Medium-light, dry, with smoky, spicy, honey notes and nutty, floral hints
Similar to Highland Park, Springbank, Bruichladdich

BRUICHLADDICH

{*brook*-LADDIE}

Bruichladdich distillery was built in 1881 by Robert, William and John Harvey using concrete, at the time a very modern form of construction, and although extended in 1975, much of the original has been sensitively retained. Its plain, whitewashed buildings are etched with dark blue and aquamarine windows and, on entering the inner courtyard through the cast iron arch, you will discover that it has a unique charm of its own. It has had several silent periods, most recently in the late 1990s. Happily, it was acquired in 2000 by a private consortium and is back in production again under a new, inspired management team – "the independent Scottish company owned by real people".

Its soft spring water filters through the hard quartz and softer sandstone of the Rhinns of Islay, emerging cold and crystal clear from a spring at Octomore that used to supply the village of Port Charlotte. The distillery operates an original nineteenth-century cast iron mash tun equipped with revolving rakes to stir the mash, 6 Oregon pine washbacks and 4 swan-necked stills. The whiskies are matured in ex-bourbon and sherry refill casks, in warehouses beside Loch Indaal.

Bruichladdich Single Islay Malt whisky, known locally as "the Laddie", is available at 10 years old (profiled), and at 15 and 20 years old. The older versions have already won medals in international competitions. It is bottled at 46%, using water from the Octomore Spring for reduction, and without any colouring, chill-filtration or homogenization. Vintage editions are also available, for example from a 1986 oloroso sherry butt. If you visit the distillery you can fill your own bottle from whatever cask is currently on tap using a valinch, a glass pipette traditionally used to draw samples.

Although all these whiskies were distilled by the previous management, considerable care goes into the cask selection for the new bottlings; the 10 years old is from 60% sherry and 40% bourbon casks, the 15 years old from

85% bourbon with 15% fresh sherry casks, and the 20 years old is from 100% bourbon casks. The whisky distilled since 2001 will not become available for a decade. In addition to Bruichladdich, it includes a new peatier version called Port Charlotte and both versions can be reserved by the cask.

The distillery welcomes visitors and offers tours and special events. You can join the Bruichladdich whisky academy and take a week's residential course, during which you will learn the skills whisky distillation and experience working with the distillery team.

Feature	Profile
●	Body
●	Sweetness
●●	Smoky
●●	Medicinal
	Tobacco
●●	Honey
●●	Spicy
●	Winey
●●	Nutty
●●	Malty
●●	Fruity
●●	Floral

Age 10 years
Strength 46%
Nose Fragrant, fruity and youthful, with a salty tang and a floral bouquet
Taste Light, medium dry with subtle complexity of honey, citrus fruits, toasted malt and almonds
Cluster I Medium-light, dry, with smoky, spicy, honey notes and nutty, floral hints
Similar to Bowmore, Isle of Jura, Springbank

BUNNAHABHAIN

{BUNNA-*hah-ven*}

Westering home with a song in the air
Light in the eye and it's goodbye to care
Laughter o'love and a welcoming there
Isle of my heart my own one.

Bunnahabhain is Gaelic for "mouth of the river". The distillery was built by William and James Greenlees in 1883 at the confluence of the Margadale River with the Sound of Islay. The site was chosen for its abundant supplies of peat and clear water, and its accessibility to the sea. The buildings are of local stone and it was once a traditional distillery community with workers' cottages and a schoolhouse.

This is one of the few distilleries that offers accommodation. Visitors can rent one of the cottages, soak up the atmosphere and enjoy the spectacular views across to the Paps of Jura. The label on the bottle depicts a mariner at the helm of his ship, happily sighting Bunnahabhain as he threads through

the Sound of Islay on his way home to Oban or Glasgow, and singing the traditional Scottish ballad "Westering Home".

Bunnahabhain is an excellent example of why the traditional method of regional classification no longer applies. Its whisky used to be heavily peated because local peat fuelled the kilns, and it was therefore typically Islay. However, early in the twentieth century Bunnahabhain departed from this tradition, and its malted barley is now supplied lightly peated. This explains why it is sometimes described as the most "Speyside" malt from Islay.

The process water is collected in a reservoir from Margadale Springs and piped to the distillery. Bunnahabhain operates a stainless steel mash tun, 6 Oregon pine washbacks, and 4 large stills – the wash stills are onion-shaped whereas the spirit stills are smaller and more pear-shaped. The whisky is matured in ex-bourbon casks, with a smaller proportion of ex-sherry European oak casks. It is reduced at the distillery to 63.5% using process water and married in vats for at least six months before bottling.

Bunnahabhain Single Islay Malt whisky is available at 12 years old (profiled) and in special editions. It is used extensively in the company's Black Bottle Islay blend, and also in Cutty Sark and Famous Grouse.

Tours and tastings are available on weekdays during summer, and by appointment at other times.

Feature	Profile
●	Body
●●	Sweetness
●	Smoky
●	Medicinal
	Tobacco
●	Honey
●	Spicy
●	Winey
●	Nutty
●●	Malty
●●	Fruity
●●●	Floral

Age 12 years
Strength 40%
Nose Aromatic and fresh, with a whiff of smoke
Taste Light, fruity and malty, with hints of honey, walnuts and spice
Cluster E Light, medium-sweet, low peat, with floral, malty notes and fruity, spicy, honey hints
Similar to Glen Moray, Glenlossie, Glenallachie

CAOL ILA

{kowel-EEL-ah}

Caol Ila is Gaelic for the "Sound of Islay", the strait that separates the islands of Islay and Jura. The distillery was founded by Hector Henderson in 1846, in a remote cove near Port Askaig on the Isle of Islay. Steamers would call twice a week to collect the whisky, and its connection with the sea is celebrated by the seal emblem on the bottle.

The distillery draws its process water from Loch nam Ban (Torrabolls Loch). It was extended in 1879 and completely modernized in 1972–4. It operates 6 stills and uses a sea-water condenser, by which the cooling water is cooled and recycled for re-use in the distillery, owing to the scarcity of water in summer. Until 1972, the *Pibroch*, a small working steamship owned by the company, delivered malting barley, coal and casks to Caol Ila's pier, and returned to Glasgow with casks of whisky. Today, malt is supplied to order from Port Ellen Maltings, and the whisky is despatched by road and ferry to the mainland.

In 1887 Alfred Barnard described its location as the wildest and most picturesque he had seen, observing that "Comfortable dwellings have been provided for the employees, forming quite a little village in themselves, and we envied the healthy life of these men and their families." There was even a Mission Hall, where services were held every Sunday for the local community. Sadly, the original stone buildings and pagoda vents have been replaced by a functional modern distillery. Yet Caol Ila still remains atmospheric, particularly on a clear winter's night

when the lights from the stillroom can be seen right across the sound to Jura.

Caol Ila whisky is used principally for the Johnnie Walker and Bell's blends. It is available in Guinness UDV's Flora and Fauna range at 15 years old (profiled) and also in the Rare Malts series at 21 years old (61.3%). A 12 years old single malt can also be obtained from Bulloch and Lade, and it is used in their export blends.

The visitor centre and shop are open all year, but appointments are advisable.

Feature	Profile
●●●	Body
●	Sweetness
●●●●	Smoky
●●	Medicinal
●	Tobacco
	Honey
●●	Spicy
	Winey
●●	Nutty
●	Malty
●	Fruity
●	Floral

Age 15 years
Strength 43%
Nose Smoky and spicy, with a whiff of the sea
Taste Peat, pepper and cigar notes, with hints of nuts, fruit and chocolate
Cluster J Full-bodied, dry, pungent, peaty and medicinal, with spicy, tobacco notes
Similar to Clynelish, Talisker, Ardbeg

CARDHU

{*car*-DOO}

ardhu is Gaelic for "Black Rock". The distillery, originally named Cardow, was one of the first to be licensed. This took place in 1824, following about ten years' operation as an illicit whisky still. The founders were John Cumming, a farmer, and his wife Helen who would fly a red flag from the barn to warn other crofters when the Excise men were searching for illicit stills. On the basis of Helen Cumming's active involvement, Cardhu claims to be the only distillery to be pioneered by a woman. Female emancipation at Cardhu did not end with Helen, however, as the Cummings' daughter-in-law Elizabeth took charge when her husband Lewis died in 1872, rebuilding it in 1885 on the present site and extending it further in 1887. For her enterprise and industry Elizabeth Cumming was known as the "Queen of the Whisky Trade".

Water is drawn from springs in the Mannoch Hills, and peat for the distillery was originally cut from Dallas Moor. Today, Cardhu operates a computer-controlled mash tun, 8 Scottish larch washbacks and 6 swan-necked copper stills. The whisky is matured in warehouses at the distillery, using only ex-bourbon American oak casks, either butts or hogsheads, which explains its light, delicate character.

Cardhu Single Malt is available at 12 years old, as featured, and at 27 years old (60%) in Guinness UDV's Rare Malts series. Cardhu whisky is also used in the Johnnie Walker blends.

The visitor centre and shop are open all year, offering guided tours. Visitors may even meet the distillery ghost, a former worker who evidently didn't want to leave!

Feature	Profile
●	Body
●●●	Sweetness
●	Smoky
	Medicinal
	Tobacco
●	Honey
●	Spicy
	Winey
●●	Nutty
●●	Malty
●●	Fruity
●●	Floral

Age 12 years
Strength 40%
Nose Fragrant, fruity and sweet
Taste Some spice, fruit, nuts and hint of smoke. Quite sweet and fresh
Cluster D Light, medium-sweet, low or no peat, with fruity, floral, malty notes and nutty hints
Similar to Aultmore, Speyside, Glengoyne

CLYNELISH

{KLINE-*leash*}

Clynelish is Sutherland's only distillery and the second most northerly of the Scottish mainland. It was established in 1819 by the Marquis of Stafford, later the first Duke of Sutherland, as an outlet for grain from his tenant farms. As such it was one of the first purpose-built distilleries, with 1 wash still and 1 spirit still, commencing production in 1821. In the mid-nineteenth century the distillery was improved and extended by George Lawson who, with his sons, combined running the distillery with farming for 50 years. At this time, Clynelish whisky was so highly prized that the distillery supplied only private customers.

The recession of 1931 forced Clynelish to close, full production not commencing again until the end of World War II. Electricity replaced coal at Clynelish in the 1960s and, in 1968, a new, modern distillery was added across the road with 6 traditional copper stills. The two distilleries operated alongside each other until 1983, when the original one was closed. During this period, the product of the original distillery was sold as "Brora" which is available in Guinness UDV's Rare Malts series at 21 years old (56.9%).

The workforce at Clynelish claim to produce their own brand of liquid gold, as the water drawn from nearby Clynemilton Burn runs over veins of gold on its way down Col-bheinn. Clynelish Single Malt whisky is available at 14 years old (profiled) in Guinness UDV's Flora and Fauna series, and at 24 years old (61.3%) in the Rare Malts series. The current whiskies are less peaty than Brora and earlier Clynelish versions. The label features a Scottish wildcat, which is the symbol of Clynelish distillery.

Visitors can be assured of a warm welcome at the distillery, which offers tours and tastings all year round. Combine a tour of Clynelish distillery with a round of golf, salmon and trout fishing on Loch Shin, or a visit to Dunrobin Castle.

Feature	Profile
●●●	Body
●●	Sweetness
●●●	Smoky
●●●	Medicinal
●	Tobacco
	Honey
●●	Spicy
	Winey
●	Nutty
●	Malty
●●	Fruity
	Floral

Age 14 years
Strength 43%
Nose Smokily fragrant, with spice and fruit
Taste Full-bodied, complex malt with peat, fruit and spice to the fore, and hints of malt, nuts and tobacco
Cluster J Full-bodied, dry, pungent, peaty and medicinal, with spicy, tobacco notes
Similar to Caol Ila, Ardbeg, Talisker

HIGHLAND
SINGLE MALT
SCOTCH WHISKY

One of the most *northerly* in *Scotland*,

CLYNELISH

distillery, was established in *Brora* by the *Marquess* of *STAFFORD* in 1819. Its building *signalled* the end of illicit *distilling* in the area and provided a ready market for locally grown *barley. Water* is piped from the *CLYNEMILTON burn* to produce this *fruity, & slightly smoky* single *MALT SCOTCH WHISKY* much appreciated by *connoisseurs*

YEARS **14** OLD

43% vol   Distilled & Bottled in SCOTLAND
CLYNELISH DISTILLERY
Brora, Sutherland, Scotland   70cl

CRAGGANMORE

*{Crag-an-*MOOR}

Cragganmore was established in 1869 by John Smith, one the most experienced of Victorian distillers, who was responsible for starting and running numerous distilleries throughout Scotland. He chose the site for its plentiful supply of cold, spring water cascading down nearby Craggan Mor. The distillery is constructed from greenstone, quarried from Craggan Mor, and it lies on a sweeping bend of the river Spey close to the railway line. Indeed, Cragganmore was one of the first to use "whisky specials" – long trains, heading south, with thousands of gallons of whisky aboard.

Cragganmore has two flat-topped spirit stills with unusual T-shaped lyne arms at the neck, and a massive new tun in the filling store that holds 60,000 litres of new spirit. The profiled malt is Cragganmore 12 years old in Guinness UDV's Classic Malts range, matured in refill casks. It is also used in the Old Parr blend. Cragganmore single malt is also available in limited editions, such as a 1984 Distillers Edition finished in port-wine casks, and a 1985 vintage matured in sherry casks (47.5%).

Visitors to Cragganmore are treated to tea or coffee on arrival, an audio-visual presentation, a guided tour of the distillery, tutored whisky nosing, and a taste of Cragganmore malt whisky to finish. The "Cragganmore Club", the converted private drawing room of a Victorian sporting lodge, adjacent to the distillery has an exhibition of Cragganmore artefacts. Visitors are welcomed from June to September, but because of the personal nature of the tour it is advisable to book in advance.

Feature	Profile
●●	Body
●●	Sweetness
●●	Smoky
	Medicinal
●	Tobacco
●●	Honey
●●	Spicy
●	Winey
●●	Nutty
●●	Malty
●	Fruity
●●●●	Floral

Age 12 years
Strength 40%
Nose Rich, medium-sweet, fragrant and flowery, with notes of herbs and smoke
Taste Medium-bodied, firm, very floral, malty with touches of peat, honey and spice
Cluster B Medium-bodied, medium-sweet, with nutty, malty, floral, honey and fruity notes
Similar to Benromach, Blair Athol, Glenturret

CRAIGELLACHIE

{*craig*-ELL-*ach-ee*}

The village of Craigellachie beside the Spey boasts three landmarks – Thomas Telford's 1815 cast-iron bridge; the Craigellachie Hotel with its famous Quaich Bar stocking 365 whiskies, one for each day of the year; and the distillery, which surveys the scene from high on the Rock of Craigellachie. Built in 1891 by Alexander Edward, rebuilt in 1896, and extended in 1965, the distillery's whisky has long been used as the heart of White Horse blends. The distillery's Victorian pagoda-topped chimney survives, but its stillroom is of modern construction, dating from 1965.

The distillery's emblem is a salmon, leaping in the Spey, which snakes along the Speyside Walk below the distillery.

Craigellachie draws its process water from springs in the Conval Hills, and uses lightly peated malted barley supplied to order. It operates a large

stainless steel Lauter mash tun, 8 Oregon pine washbacks and 4 large stills. The whisky is matured in ex-bourbon American oak casks and a few European oak sherry butts. The distillery was sold to Bacardi in 1999, and a new bottling of its malt is in prospect.

Craigellachie Single Speyside Malt whisky is available at 14 years old (profiled) in Guinness UDV's Flora and Fauna range, though this version is now difficult to find, in the Rare Malts series, and from independents such as Connoisseurs Choice. The new edition is due to become available in late-2002. The whisky is used in Dewar's White Label, 12 years old Special Reserve, and Ancestor de Luxe (43%) blends, which account for the bulk of its production.

There is no visitor centre at the distillery, but visitors are welcome by appointment.

Feature	Profile
●●	Body
●●●	Sweetness
●●	Smoky
●	Medicinal
	Tobacco
	Honey
●	Spicy
	Winey
●●	Nutty
●●	Malty
●●	Fruity
●●	Floral

Age 14 years
Strength 43%
Nose Fragrant, flowery and peaty
Taste Sweet, smoky and creamy, with citrus, nuts and malty notes and a hint of spice
Cluster H Medium-bodied, medium-sweet, with smoky, fruity, spicy notes and floral, nutty hints
Similar to Balblair, Glenmorangie, Oban

BOTTLED
2000

CONNOISSEURS
CHOICE

SPEYSIDE
Single Malt Scotch Whisky

DISTILLED AT
CRAIGELLACHIE
DISTILLERY
Proprietors: White Horse Distillers Ltd

DISTILLED
1987

Specially selected, produced
and bottled by
Gordon & MacPhail
Elgin Scotland
Product of Scotland

70cl   40% vol

DAILUAINE

{*dal*-YOO-*in*}

Dailuaine distillery was founded by William Mackenzie in 1851, and its name is Gaelic for "the green vale". The distillery nestles in a pretty spot beside the Carron Burn, between Ben Rinnes and the River Spey. Its granite buildings are late-Victorian, and are nicely preserved despite a major fire in 1917. Until the 1950s the distillery was powered by an ingenious combination of two water wheels, coupled by an overhead chain, and four steam engines.

For more that a century, Dailuaine received its supplies and despatched its whisky by rail. The steam locomotive *Dailuaine No. 1* was in use until 1967 and is still preserved as a feature at Aberfeldy distillery in Perthshire. The distillery was converted to electricity in the 1950s and now operates 6 pot stills using natural gas steam heating.

Dailuaine draws its process water mashing from the Bailliemullich Burn, and cooling water from the Carron Burn, all of which are fed by springs from Ben Rinnes. The emblem on the label is a badger, because badger setts are to be found in the woods nearby.

The whisky is matured in a combination of bourbon and sherry casks. Most is used in Johnnie Walker blends, though the 16 years old Dailuaine Single Malt (profiled) is available in Guinness UDV's Flora and Fauna series, in the Rare Malts series at 22 years old (60.9%) and from some independents.

Dailuaine does not have a visitor centre or offer tours.

Feature	Profile
●●●●	Body
●●	Sweetness
●●	Smoky
	Medicinal
	Tobacco
●	Honey
●●	Spicy
●●	Winey
●●	Nutty
●●	Malty
●●	Fruity
●	Floral

Age 16 years
Strength 43%
Nose Fruity and aromatic, quite sherried and malty
Taste Full-bodied, strongly sherried with nutty, smoky and spicy notes
Cluster A Full-bodied, medium-sweet, pronounced sherry with fruity, spicy, malty notes and nutty, smoky hints
Similar to Royal Lochnagar, Dalmore, Mortlach

SPEYSIDE
SINGLE MALT SCOTCH WHISKY

DAILUAINE

is the GAELIC for "the green vale". The distillery, established in 1852, lies in a hollow by the CARRON BURN in BANFFSHIRE. The Single Malt Scotch Whisky has a full bodied fruity nose and a smoky finish. For more than a hundred years all distillery supplies were despatched by rail. The steam locomotive "DAILUAINE NO.1" was in use from 1939 – 1967 and is preserved on the STRATHSPEY RAILWAY.

AGED **16** YEARS

DALMORE

{*dall*-MORE}

Dalmore is Norse for "big meadowland" and the distillery was built in 1839 by Alexander Matheson in fine barley growing country, on the site of a former meal mill. It sits in a beautiful spot opposite the Black Isle – not actually an island, but a peninsula of the Cromarty Firth. The area is teeming with wildlife, with porpoises in the Firth, a buzzard's nest in the firs, and herons on the shore. Many original Victorian buildings remain, with the pagoda-topped malting kiln as a centrepiece, though in 1966 the distillery was extended. In World War I it was requisitioned by the Americans for the production of deep sea mines, and they added the "Yankie" pier. Another feature is a Victorian steam engine from 1898.

The emblem on the label features the stag's head of the Mackenzie clan, as the Mackenzie whisky family owned Dalmore for over 80 years. Legend has it that Alexander III awarded the stag's head to the clan when Mackenzie saved him from a charging wounded stag. Dalmore whisky is favoured in cigar-smoking circles, so a "Cigar Malt" was produced to foster this association. It is also an excellent "after-dinner" malt.

The distillery draws soft clear water from the River Averon (river of tears), and operates a stainless steel mash tun, 8 Oregon pine washbacks, 2 large and 2 small wash stills encased in copper cooling jackets to increase reflux, and 2 large and 2 small flat-topped spirit stills. Production is quite high at 3.5 million litres (6.2 million pints) a year, most of which goes for blending. The whisky is matured in a mixture of first fill ex-bourbon American oak and specially selected aged oloroso sherry casks, stored in warehouses at the site and married in sherry butts prior to bottling.

The Dalmore Highland Malt Scotch whisky is available at 12 years old (profiled), at 21 years old, and as an unaged "Cigar Malt". There are special editions, 30, 52 and 60 years old.

The visitor centre is open all year. It has a shop and offers tours and tastings, though appointments are necessary.

Feature	Profile
●●●	Body
●●	Sweetness
●●	Smoky
●	Medicinal
	Tobacco
●	Honey
●●	Spicy
●●	Winey
●	Nutty
●●	Malty
●●●	Fruity
●	Floral

Age 12 years
Strength 40%
Nose Rich, fruity and sherried, with a nutty, orange/marzipan note and a whiff of smoke
Taste Medium-bodied, malt and marmalade, with some peat and sherry notes and a hint of salt
Cluster A Full-bodied, medium-sweet, pronounced sherry with fruity, spicy, malty notes and nutty, smoky hints
Similar to Royal Lochnagar, Dailuaine, Mortlach

DALWHINNIE

{*dal*-WHIN-*ee*}

Dalwhinnie is Gaelic for "meeting place", and stands at a point on an old Highland road where cattle drovers would meet and rest. The distillery was built by Alexander Mackenzie in 1897 and started production in 1898, only to close almost immediately. Its location – a "desolate, wind-sliced, rain-lashed patch of Highland wilderness"– was chosen for the abundant supply of clear, Highland spring water, ample peat for the fire, and its proximity to the Highland Railway line.

The distillery was sold several times before 1926, when it was acquired by the Distillers Company, now part of Guinness UDV. It was rebuilt in 1938 following a major fire, modernised in the 1970s and refurbished in the 1990s when a visitor centre was added. The 1930s stone buildings are white-faced with slate roofs and twin pagoda-topped chimneys, set against a stark backdrop of the snow-capped heather hills of Drumochter Pass and the Athol Forest. It is certainly Scotland's highest distillery and probably the coldest too.

It doubles as a Met Office weather station and in 1994 recorded the lowest average temperature of any inhabited part of Britain at 6° C.

Its snow-melted water collects at 2,000 feet (610 metres) in Lochan an Doire-Uaine and then runs through peat and purple heather into the distillery burn, Allt an t'Sluic. In earlier times the barley was malted over a fire of locally-cut peat, but today it is supplied to order by Roseisle maltsters. The distillery operates a stainless steel mash tun, 1 Oregon pine and 5 Siberian larch washbacks, and 2 large onion-shaped stills. Somewhat unusually, the spirit is still condensed in traditional copper worms housed in large wooden tubs at the front of the still house (right of picture). The whisky is matured in ex-bourbon American oak casks, taking longer than normal due to the altitude and humidity.

Dalwhinnie Single Highland Malt is available at 15 years old (profiled) in Guinness UDV's Classic Malts range, and in limited editions such as a double-matured 1985 vintage finished

in oloroso sherry casks. Richard Joynson, of Loch Fyne Whiskies, described it as "exotic white lingerie (pure, with a distinctly racy streak)". Indeed an earlier label declared it "an elegant malt whisky with a heathery, lacy finish", and it is an excellent accompaniment to rich desserts such as a black forest gâteau or sticky toffee pudding and cream (enough said).

The visitor centre attracts 50,000 visitors a year and offers tours, tastings and a shop.

Feature	Profile
●●	Body
●●	Sweetness
●●	Smoky
	Medicinal
	Tobacco
●●	Honey
●	Spicy
	Winey
●	Nutty
●●	Malty
●●	Fruity
●●	Floral

Age 15 years
Strength 43%
Nose Sweet, nutty aroma with a floral edge hinting of smoke and marmalade
Taste Fresh and heathery with fruit and honey notes and a whiff of peat
Cluster C Medium-bodied, medium-sweet, with fruity, floral, honey, malty notes and spicy hints
Similar to Benriach, Glen Elgin, Balvenie

DEANSTON

{DEANS-*ton*}

Deanston distillery was originally a cotton mill, built in 1785 by Richard Arkwright who invented the "spinning jenny", and several of its buildings date from that period. It lies beside the river Teith near Castle Doune in Perthshire. The mill was originally driven by water power, but it was converted to a distillery in 1965 which is powered by hydro-electric turbines that also contribute surplus electricity to the national grid. It retains some interesting listed buildings, including a magnificent vaulted weaving shed now used as a maturation warehouse. The water that supplies the distillery and drives its turbines is diverted from the Teith by a canal, and returned to the river through a network of Victorian water caverns that are home to a colony of bats.

Deanston distillery draws its water from the river Teith and uses un-peated malted barley, though the mashing water contains enough peaty traces to account for a slightly smoky note in the finished whisky. It operates a large open cast iron mash tun, 8 stainless steel washbacks and 4 medium sized pot stills. The whisky is matured in a range of American and European oak refill casks, and also some fresh sherry butts that will contribute more winey flavours to future versions.

Deanston Single Highland Malt whisky is available at 12 years old (profiled), and at 17 and 25 years old. Special vintage editions are

occasionally produced, such as a 1967 cask-strength whisky that was bottled in 2002. The whisky is also used in Drumgray Highland Liquor, which won gold medals in 1993 and 1999, and Wallace Single Malt Scotch Whisky Liqueur.

Deanston does not have a visitor centre.

Feature	Profile
●●	Body
●●	Sweetness
●	Smoky
	Medicinal
	Tobacco
●●	Honey
●	Spicy
●	Winey
●	Nutty
●●●	Malty
●●	Fruity
●	Floral

Age 12 years
Strength 40%
Nose Fragrant and honeyed with a malty, cereal note
Taste Malty and fruity, with a hint of spice and a sweet aftertaste
Cluster F Medium-bodied, medium-sweet, low peat, malty notes and sherry, honey, spicy hints
Similar to Ardmore, Auchroisk, Glenrothes

DUFFTOWN

{DUFF-*ton*}

Dufftown distillery was converted from a meal mill in 1896 by Peter MacKenzie and Richard Stackpole. It is a pretty Victorian stone distillery nestling in rolling hills and woodland beside the River Dullan, a subsidiary of the Spey. The distillery's emblem is a kingfisher, and examples of these can be seen fishing for trout nearby.

Its water is drawn from Highland John's Well, an excellent source of pure spring water that rises in the Conval Hills about four miles from the distillery, and which has never been known to fail even in the driest summer. The ownership of the well was initially hotly disputed, to the extent that rival distillers would venture out in the dead of night to divert and re-divert its course, but this was eventually decided in Dufftown's favour early in the twentieth century.

The distillery was extended in 1968, in 1980 and again in 1999 to its present capacity. It now operates a stainless steel mash tun, 12 stainless steel washbacks and 6 stills, using a complex distillation that is capable of producing over 4 million litres (7 million pints) of spirit a year. The single malt is matured in Spanish sherry and American bourbon casks, whereas refill casks are used for the whisky intended for blending.

Most of the production is used in Bell's 8 years old blend. The single malt is available in Guinness UDV's Flora and Fauna range at 15 years old (profiled), and in the Rare Malts series at 21 years old (54.8%). It is also available at various vintages from independent bottlings.

Dufftown distillery does not have a visitor centre or offer tours.

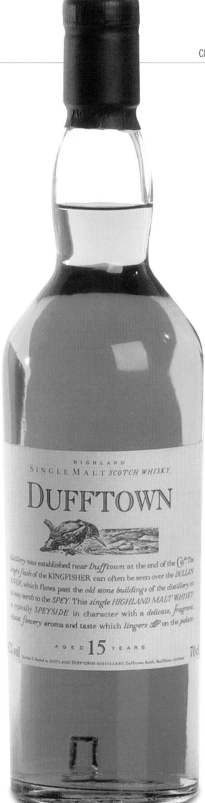

Feature	Profile
●●	Body
●●●	Sweetness
●	Smoky
●	Medicinal
	Tobacco
	Honey
	Spicy
	Winey
●	Nutty
●●	Malty
●●	Fruity
●●	Floral

Age 15 years
Strength 43%
Nose Sweet, fragrant and fruity aroma
Taste Medium-bodied with flowers, fruit and malty flavours, and a hint of smoke
Cluster G Medium-bodied, sweet, low peat and floral notes
Similar to Glenfiddich, Miltonduff, Speyburn

EDRADOUR

{*edra*-DOWER}

Edradour is the classic example of a farm distillery, the smallest in Scotland and run by three men. If you want to see an example of what whisky distillation was like in the nineteenth century, then this is it. Established in 1825 as a farmers' co-operative, the present buildings were constructed by the Duke of Athol and date from 1837. Little has changed here in the past 160 years, the last major modernisation being in 1947 when the water wheel was replaced by electricity.

Its water flows down granite hills and through the peat of Moulin Moor, before rising clear and cold a short distance above the distillery. Everything about Edradour is small. It operates a cast iron mash tun with a capacity of only one ton of barley, 2 Oregon pine washbacks, and 2 tiny stills. The still

house is roughly the size of your living room, and the spirit still is the smallest allowed under Excise regulations – any smaller and it could be hidden away in a hillside; and indeed they were in the eighteenth century, as this is an area rich in smuggling lore. The whiskies are matured European oloroso sherry casks, the latter being specially selected annually in Spain.

The output at Edradour is tiny too, distilling in a year what a typical Speyside distillery produces in a week. Edradour's biggest statistic is the number of visitors who flock here to experience the charm of a traditional farm distillery set in pretty gardens, and the warm welcome of the visitor centre staff, who outnumber the production team.

Edradour Single Highland Malt whisky is only available at 10 years old (profiled). It is a hand-crafted malt whisky, unique and difficult to find, but well worth the hunt. An aroma "like stepping into a Dickensian sweet shop" as Graham Nown described it, and this could equally apply to the distillery itself.

The visitor centre, a converted malt barn, and shop are open all year. Tours include an audio-visual presentation, exhibition of traditional whisky-making, and a free tasting.

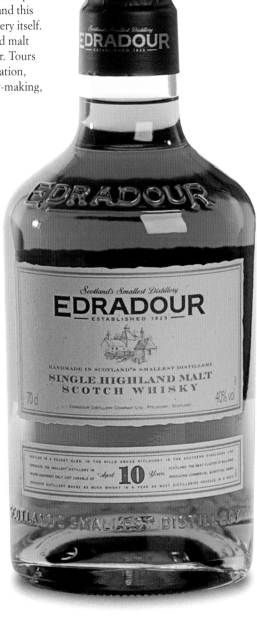

Feature	Profile
●●	Body
●●●	Sweetness
●	Smoky
	Medicinal
	Tobacco
●●	Honey
●	Spicy
●	Winey
●●●●	Nutty
●●	Malty
●●	Fruity
●●	Floral

Age 10 years
Strength 40%
Nose Fragrant and honeyed, like sugared almonds, with a whiff of smoke
Taste Sweet and creamy, some fruit and malt notes, and hints of sherry and spice
Cluster B Medium-bodied, medium-sweet, with nutty, malty, floral, honey and fruity notes
Similar to Strathisla, Longmorn, Knockando

GLENALLACHIE

{*glen*-ALLACH-*ee*}

Glenallachie distillery was built in 1967 beside the Lour Burn above Aberlour by Charles Mackinlay & Co. to a functional design by the architect William Delmé Evans, and is typical of 1960s single level distillery architecture. The cooling water is drawn from ponds created by a dam in the river fed from a small waterfall, and this provides the distillery's most attractive feature. The warm water from the condensers is piped back to the ponds which gives them a steamy look in winter and is enjoyed by a colony of ducks that are included in the inventory.

The distillery draws its water from deep granite springs and snow-fed burns on Ben Rinnes and uses lightly-peated malted barley. It operates a stainless steel semi-Lauter mash tun, 2 stainless steel washbacks and 4 medium-sized pot stills. The wash stills have pinched waists while the spirit stills follow the more usual onion shape. The whisky is matured in ex-bourbon American oak casks and refills.

Glenallachie Single Highland Malt whisky is available at 12 years old (profiled) from Delhaize Le Lion, part of the Pernod Ricard group. It is also bottled as vintages by Signatory, and is used in 12 years old Clan Campbell, 18 years old Legendary and White Heather blends.

Glenallachie distillery does not have a visitor centre or offer tours.

Feature	Profile
●	Body
●●●	Sweetness
●	Smoky
	Medicinal
	Tobacco
●	Honey
●	Spicy
	Winey
●	Nutty
●●	Malty
●●	Fruity
●●	Floral

Age 12 years
Strength 40%
Nose Aromatic, fresh and malty
Taste Light but well-balanced, with floral, vanilla and apple notes, and a long sweet finish
Cluster E Light, medium-sweet, low peat, with floral, malty notes and fruity, spicy, honey hints
Similar to Glenlossie, Glenkinchie, Inchgower

GLEN DEVERON

{*glen*-DEV-*er-en*}

Macduff distillery was built in 1959 on the outskirts of Macduff, a small fishing town and seaside resort on the east bank of the River Deveron, opposite the ancient Royal burgh of Banff.

It draws its process water from springs above the distillery and its cooling water (when necessary) from the River Deveron, which gives its name to the malt whisky although it can also be found as Macduff. Lightly peated, malted barley is delivered to order, and a mixture of distillers' culture and brewers' yeasts is used in the fermentation. The distillery operates a stainless steel mash tun, 9 stainless steel washbacks, 2 wash stills and 3 spirit stills. The whisky is matured in warehouses beside the Deveron in bourbon, sherry and refill casks, some of which are charred in the distillery's own cooperage to add toasty, vanilla flavours.

Glen Deveron Single Highland Malt whisky is available at 10 years old (profiled), at 5 years old for export only, and as Macduff versions bottled by Connoisseurs Choice, Cadenhead and Signatory. It is also used in William Lawson's Finest Scotch Whisky and 12 years old Scottish Gold blends.

Macduff distillery does not have a visitor centre or offer tours.

Aerial view of Macduff distillery beside the River Deveron, home of Glen Deveron Malt and William Lawson's blends.

Feature	Profile
● ●	Body
● ● ●	Sweetness
●	Smoky
●	Medicinal
●	Tobacco
●	Honey
●	Spicy
● ●	Winey
	Nutty
● ●	Malty
	Fruity
●	Floral

Age 10 years
Strength 40%
Nose Fresh, sweet and malty, with a sherry note and a hint of sea air
Taste Medium-bodied, honey and spice notes, some oaky vanilla and a soft smoky finish
Cluster F Medium-bodied, medium-sweet, low peat, malty notes and sherry, honey, spicy hints
Similar to Tomatin, Glenrothes

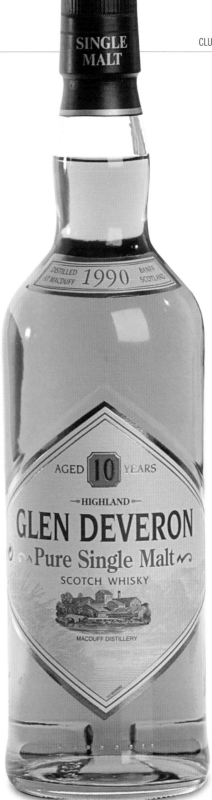

GLENDRONACH

{*glen*-DRON-*ach*}

lendronach, Gaelic for "valley of the blackberries", is a small distillery nestling in the Valley of Forgue, near the town of Huntly on the eastern edge of Speyside. Whisky has been made here since 1826, when James Allardyce joined with local whisky-makers to found the company, but they had probably been distilling whisky illegally for several years prior to that.

The distillery still uses traditional washbacks made from solid Oregon pine, and the original copper coal-fired kilns have remained unchanged since the nineteenth century. Unlike many other distilleries, Glendronach's barley is still turned by hand on the malting floor, and visitors can view the maturation warehouse where the malt whisky, profiled here, is aged for at least

15 years on earthen floors. Indeed, Glendronach oozes tradition, and there is an atmosphere of timeless industry and contentment here. The original buildings surround an old cobbled courtyard, and a welcome is assured both from the staff and the resident rooks. Legend has it, that so long as the rooks remain, Glendronach will enjoy good fortune – for in the old days, it was the rooks that first warned of approaching Excise officers!

The immense sherry flavour of Glendronach 15 years old malt whisky derives from its long maturation in specially selected Spanish sherry casks.

The distillery offers guided tours all year, a video presentation and a shop. Overnight accommodation is also available.

Feature	Profile
●●●●	Body
●●	Sweetness
●●	Smoky
	Medicinal
	Tobacco
●●	Honey
●	Spicy
●●●●	Winey
●●	Nutty
●●	Malty
●●	Fruity
	Floral

Age 15 years
Strength 40%
Nose Big sherry aroma,
followed by spicy smoke
Taste Complex, full sherry,
malty-toffee flavour, moderately
peated with honey and fruit
notes
Cluster A Full-bodied, medium-
sweet, pronounced sherry with
fruity, spicy, malty notes and
nutty, smoky hints
Similar to Macallan, Dailuaine,
Royal Lochnagar

GLENDULLAN

{*glen*-DULL-*an*}

Old Glendullan distillery was built in Dufftown in 1897 by William Williams and Sons. It was the seventh distillery to be built in Dufftown, and thus was coined the local saying "Rome was built of seven hills and Dufftown stands on seven stills".

All its machinery was powered by a 14ft (4.3 metres) water wheel driven by water from the River Fiddich, until after World War II. *Harper's Weekly* reported in 1897 "This water power will be a great saving compared to steam engines". A private railway line, linked to Dufftown Station and shared with its sister distillery Mortlach, was used to deliver supplies and despatch the whisky to Aberdeen.

Distillation commenced in April 1898, the whisky was initially used for the Williams' blends. In 1902 Glendullan whisky became a favourite of King Edward VII and, in 1995, it was chosen for the "Houses of Parliament" exclusive single malt by the then Speaker, Betty Boothroyd.

A modern distillery was added in 1972 next to "Old Glendullan", and for a while they ran in tandem. The new design, which was successfully repeated at several other distilleries, is unattractive but proved to be much more efficient and so the old distillery ceased production in 1985 and is now used for engineering work.

Glendullan distillery draws its process water from Goatswell Spring and its cooling water from the River Fiddich. It operates a 12 tonne copper-topped mash tun, 8 Oregon pine washbacks and 6 stills. The spirit stills are larger than the wash stills, which is rather unusual. The whisky is matured in oak refill casks, the bulk of its production now being used in Guinness UDV's and Old Parr blends.

Glendullan Single Malt whisky is available in the Guinness UDV's Flora and Fauna range at 12 years old (profiled), and also in the Rare Malts series at 23 years old (63.1%). Other vintages are available through independent bottlers.

It does not have a visitor centre.

Feature	Profile
●●●	Body
●●	Sweetness
●	Smoky
	Medicinal
	Tobacco
●●	Honey
●	Spicy
●●	Winey
●	Nutty
●●	Malty
●●●	Fruity
●●	Floral

Age 12 years
Strength 43%
Nose Fruity, malty and honeyed with hints of sherry and vanilla oak
Taste Firm and mellow with fruity, honey and malty notes and a floral finish
Cluster C Medium-bodied, medium-sweet, with fruity, floral, honey, malty notes and spicy hints
Similar to Balvenie, Glenlivet, Linkwood

SPEYSIDE
SINGLE MALT
SCOTCH WHISKY

GLENDULLAN

distillery, located in a beautiful *wooded* valley was ⅍ built in 1897 and is one of seven established in *Dufftown* in the C19ᵃ. The *River Fiddich* flows past the *distillery*; originally *providing power* to drive machinery, it is now used ⅍ for cooling. *GLENDULLAN* is a firm, mellow *single MALT SCOTCH WHISKY* with a fruity bouquet and a smooth *lingering* finish.

AGED **12** YEARS

43% vol

Distilled & Bottled in SCOTLAND
GLENDULLAN DISTILLERY
Dufftown, Keith, Banffshire, Scotland

70cl

GLEN ELGIN

{*glen*-ELG-*in*}

Glen Elgin distillery was built near Elgin in 1898 by William Simpson and James Carle, and to a design by the architect Charles Doig. It commenced production in May 1900. The recession in the whisky industry, which followed that year, meant this was the last distillery to be built on Speyside for sixty years. The site was originally chosen for its proximity to Glen Burn and Longmorn station. The distillery was lit by paraffin and powered by water until electricity was installed in the 1950s. It draws its water from springs below Millbuies Loch.

Glen Elgin was rebuilt in 1964, with a new mash-house and still house, and steam heating replaced the coal-fired boilers in 1970. It uses unpeated malted barley and uses a stainless steel Lauter mash tun, 6 larch washbacks and 6 swan-necked stills. The malt whisky is matured in American oak bourbon casks, refills, and a few European ex-sherry casks.

Glen Elgin Single Malt is available at 12 years old (profiled) in Guinness UDV's Flora and Fauna range, and from some independents. It is the heart of White Horse and Bell's Extra Special blends, which take 95 per cent of its production. The emblem on the bottle is the house martin, because several pairs faithfully return ever year to raise their young under the eaves of the distillery buildings. The distillery does not have a visitor centre or offer tours.

Six traditional condensers, each consisting of a copper worm immersed in a tub of cold running water, are still in use at Glen Elgin distillery.

Feature	Profile
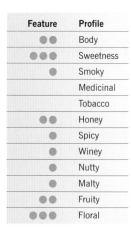 ●●	Body
●●●	Sweetness
●	Smoky
	Medicinal
	Tobacco
●●	Honey
●	Spicy
●	Winey
●	Nutty
●	Malty
●●	Fruity
●●●	Floral

Age 12 years
Strength 43%
Nose Honeyed aroma and a whiff of smoke
Taste Aromatic, fresh and fruity, with grassy sweetness
Cluster C Medium-bodied, medium-sweet, with fruity, floral, honey, malty notes and spicy hints
Similar to Glenlivet, Dalwhinnie, Knockando

SPEYSIDE
SINGLE MALT
SCOTCH WHISKY

GLEN ELGIN

founded in 1898 in the *parish of LONGMORN*, *has grown* over *the years* and is now a *sizeable distillery. For as long as can be remembered.* *HOUSE MARTINS return every APRIL to raise their young under the eaves of the distillery buildings. Springs rising near MILLBUIES LOCH* provide the water used *to produce this deep amber, honied, single MALT SCOTCH WHISKY.*

AGED **12** YEARS

43% vol   70cl

Distilled & Bottled in SCOTLAND.
GLEN ELGIN DISTILLERY
Longmorn, Elgin, Moray, Scotland.

GLENFARCLAS

{*glen*-FAR-*class*}

Glenfarclas distillery, in the "valley of the green grass".

Glenfarclas distillery in Speyside is one of the few to have remained in private ownership since it was founded in 1836 by Robert Hay. Six generations of the Grant family have distilled whisky here. Glenfarclas means "the valley of the green grass" and the distillery stands in the meadows at the foot of Ben Rinnes, drawing its soft water from springs that flow through granite and heather into the valley.

The distillery was rebuilt in 1897 and further extended and modernized in the 1960s. The 6 stills at Glenfarclas are amongst the largest on Speyside, with the big wash still holding nearly 30,000 litres.

Glenfarclas supplies at least 6 whiskies, of cask ages ranging from 10 years old (profiled) through 12, 15, 21, 25 and 30 years old. Their cask-strength "105" malt whisky bears no age statement; and there is also a limited supply of a 40 year old still available. The extensive range of Glenfarclas malts allows for detailed research on the effect of barrel maturation.

Glenfarclas malt whiskies are now aged mainly in sherry casks, using a mixture of first-fill and refill, although this has not always been the case. This contributes to the malt's pronounced sherry character, particularly in the newer malts where new sherry casks have been most recently deployed. The

The distillery workforce of 1891.

10 year old is a straw gold in colour, delicately light, sweet and malty, with a floral, fruity nose and leaving a long slightly spicy finish. It is a whisky of high quality, strongly to be recommended.

Glenfarclas visitor centre features the splendid "Ships Room", which is fitted out with the original oak panelling and ship's furniture of the *Empress of Australia*, 1913–52. The visitor centre and shop are open all year for tours and tastings.

Feature	Profile
●●	Body
●●●●	Sweetness
●	Smoky
	Medicinal
	Tobacco
●	Honey
●●	Spicy
●●●	Winey
●●	Nutty
●●●	Malty
●●	Fruity
●●	Floral

Age 10 years
Strength 40%
Nose Light, estery and floral
Taste Sweetly sherried with a creamy, nutty flavour and showing some spice and fruit
Cluster B Medium-bodied, medium-sweet, with nutty, malty, floral, honey and fruity notes
Similar to Glenturret, Blair Athol, Strathisla

GLENFIDDICH

*{glen-*FID-*ich}*

Glenfiddich is Gaelic for "valley of the deer". The distillery, which was founded in 1886 by William and Elizabeth Grant, started production on Christmas Day 1887 and has been continuously owned and managed by the Grant family for five generations. The Grants are one of the few whisky dynasties to have successfully resisted the conglomerates.

All the water used at Glenfiddich, from mashing to bottling, is drawn from a single source – the Robbie Dhu Spring – a fact unmatched by any other producer. Hence their marketing slogan "a single source of inspiration" and their claim to be the "château-bottled" malt whisky in Scotland. Flowing from the Conval Hills through peat and granite, the water is soft and peaty. The distillery uses lightly-peated malted barley and operates 2 stainless steel mash tuns, 24 Douglas fir washbacks, and 28 stills.

The pot spirit stills are unusually small, being faithful reproductions of the original 3 stills bought second-hand by William Grant in 1886. The stills used to be directly heated by coal fires, with rummagers to remove burnt solids and burnish the interiors. This increases the exposure of the low wines to copper and thus enhances the flavour of the spirit. Direct flame heating and rummagers were partly replaced by steam heating in 1993, however, and this may affect the flavour of future whiskies.

Glenfiddich Special Reserve was the first to be sold internationally, as an un-aged single malt in the mid 1960s. This probably explains why the 12 years old is now the world's best-selling single malt whisky and is available in about 200 countries. Its pale golden colour and delicate flavour derive from the use of lightly-peated malt, the pure, soft Robbie Dhu water, and maturation principally in American ex-bourbon oak casks.

Glenfiddich also produces an unusual vatted malt from whiskies matured for 15 years in American bourbon casks and Spanish or Portugese ex-oloroso sherry casks. Some of the matured whisky is transferred to new, unprepared oak casks for a few months. The whiskies from all three types of cask are then married in a large Solera European oak vat, which is always kept at least half full. The newer whiskies thus combine with older ones and the resulting vatted malt is drawn off into marrying tuns for a further six month's maturation. Because the Solera vat is always at least half full, its reservoir of older whiskies continues to mature indefinitely. The result is Glenfiddich Solera Reserve, a delightfully complex, multi-dimensional single malt whisky at least 15 years old, with vanilla, fruit, cream and sherry highlights.

Glenfiddich also produces an 18 years old Ancient Reserve, a 21 years old Millennium Reserve, a Vintage Reserve, 30 and 40 years old versions, a Malt Whisky Liqueur, a 50 years old malt and a Vintage 1937 edition.

Glenfiddich distillery has an excellent visitor centre offering an audio-visual film in six languages, guided tours, whisky tastings in the Malt Barn, and a well-stocked shop. It is the only distillery where visitors can view the whole production process, from mashing the barley malt to bottling the whisky. It is open all year and is definitely worth a visit.

Feature	Profile
●	Body
●●●	Sweetness
●	Smoky
	Medicinal
	Tobacco
	Honey
	Spicy
	Winey
	Nutty
●●	Malty
●●	Fruity
●●	Floral

Age 12 years
Strength 40%
Nose Light, fresh and fragrant with a touch of pine
Taste Medium-sweet with a delicate harmony of malty, citric and floral flavours and a hint of peat
Cluster G Medium-bodied, sweet, low peat and floral notes
Similar to Dufftown, Glen Spey, Speyburn

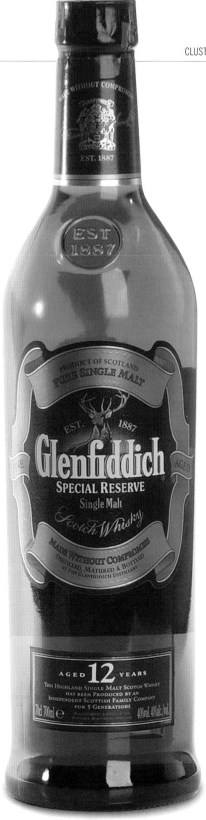

GLEN GARIOCH

{glen-GEAR-ee}

Glen Garioch distillery is one of the oldest in Scotland. It definitely existed in 1797 under Thomas Simpson, but other records suggest it was operating in 1785. It was extended to 3 stills in 1973 and has suffered several periods of closure, most recently in the mid 1990s. Happily, this charming distillery in the Aberdeenshire village of Old Meldrum, was refurbished by the present owners and reopened in 1997. It boasts some fine Victorian granite buildings with traditional floor maltings, topped by twin pagoda chimneys.

The distillery draws its water from springs on Percock Hill, and it is used to operate its own floor maltings with peat cut locally from Pitsligo Moss, but these were discontinued in 1997. The present malt is, therefore, fairly heavily peated, unusually so for a Speyside malt, but should be much less peaty in future editions.

The distillery operates a stainless steel mash tun, 8 stainless steel washbacks, 1 wash still and 2 smaller spirit stills. The whisky is matured in a mixture of ex-bourbon American oak and ex-sherry European oak casks, in warehouses at the site.

In addition to the 15 years old (profiled), Glen Garioch is also available at 8 years old and 21 years old, and in special cask-strength bottlings at 18 years old (59.4%), at 27 years old (49.6%) and at 29 years old (57.5%). There is also a range of 21 years old vatted malts from specially selected casks sold in ceramic bottles, and a 200th Anniversary malt distilled in 1961 that was bottled in 1996. The whiskies have won several awards in international competitions, especially the 21 years old which has won two gold medals.

Glen Garioch distillery does not have a visitor centre or offer tours.

Feature	Profile
●●	Body
●	Sweetness
●●●	Smoky
	Medicinal
	Tobacco
	Honey
●●●	Spicy
●	Winey
	Nutty
●●	Malty
●●	Fruity
●●	Floral

Age 15 years
Strength 43%
Nose Heather fire smoke, together with lavender and a whiff of sherry
Taste Complex oak and raisin notes, with smoke, spices and malt
Cluster H Medium-bodied, medium-sweet, with smoky, fruity, spicy notes and floral, nutty hints
Similar to Teaninich, Glenmorangie

GLENGOYNE

{*glen*-GOY'*n*}

Burnfoot distillery probably operated illegally in the early part of the nineteenth century, gaining its first licence to distil whisky in 1833. It was renamed "Glen Guin", or "the valley of the wild geese", when Lang Brothers bought it in 1876. While there has been some modernization over the years, it retains a nineteenth-century charm. It nestles prettily in a wooded valley below Dumgoyne hill, from which the Glengoyne Burn courses through sandstone and over a spectacular 15 metre (49 feet) waterfall, eventually flowing into Loch Lomond.

Glengoyne distillery draws its soft process water from Lock Carron and its cooling water from the Glengoyne Burn. It uses only Scottish barley, Golden Promise and Chariot varieties, air dried after germination and hence unpeated. The carton boldly states "Scotland's Unpeated Malt" which is the whisky's signature. The distillery operates a medium-sized copper domed mash tun, 6 Oregon pine washbacks, 1 wash still and 2 smaller spirit stills with boil balls in the necks. The size and shape of the spirit stills and boil balls contribute greatly through catalysis and reflux to the flavour of the resulting spirit. The whisky is matured in a combination of refill and sherry casks, in dunnage warehouses at the site. When the malts are vatted, none of Glengoyne's distinctive flavours and aromas is allowed to dominate. The result is that each expresses itself fully in a refined, subtle balance of flavours.

Glengoyne Single Highland Malt whisky is available at 10 years old (profiled) and at 17, 21 and 30 years old. Several single cask vintages have been produced, for example, Autumn 1969, Spring 1972 and 1971 Vintage

bottlings. Limited editions are produced, such as a Millennium edition in 2000, a 16 years old Scottish oak edition in 2001, and it is also used in blends such as Cutty Sark, Famous Grouse and Lang's Supreme.

Glengoyne's heritage centre, a converted nineteenth-century warehouse, is less than 12 miles from Glasgow. It is open all year and offers an audio-visual film about the history of the distillery, guided tours, tastings and a shop. There are also evening nosing sessions, for which advanced booking is necessary.

Feature	Profile
●	Body
●●	Sweetness
	Smoky
	Medicinal
	Tobacco
●	Honey
●	Spicy
●	Winey
●●	Nutty
●●	Malty
●●●	Fruity
●●	Floral

Age 10 years
Strength 40%
Nose Rich malty aroma with honeysuckle and sherry
Taste Oak, apple and butter notes, hints of sherry and spice, and a long fruity finish
Cluster D Light, medium-sweet, low or no peat, with fruity, floral, malty notes and nutty hints
Similar to Auchentoshan, Cardhu, Glen Grant

125

GLEN GRANT

{*glen*-GRANT}

Glen Grant distillery was founded in 1840 by brothers John and James Grant, who were among the first to be licensed in the Scottish Highlands. The distillery's most famous owner was James Grant's son, Major James Grant, who travelled extensively in India and southern Africa at the end of the nineteenth century. Major Grant's Victorian garden boasts a fine collection of woodland plants, mature orchards, a lily pond and rare exotic plants from around the world. Although the distillery has been substantially extended, many of the original buildings remain, clustered around the Grants' nineteenth-century house with its turrets, gables and courtyard – a fine example of the old Scottish Baronial style.

The distillery's water is drawn from the Caperdonich Spring, supplemented by the Back Burn. Its malted barley is supplied unpeated from specialist maltsters, and the distillery operates a stainless steel mash tun, 10 Oregon pine washbacks, 4 wash stills and 4 spirit stills. Fermentation takes 48 hours, using only distillers' yeast. The bulbous stills incorporate an unusual boil ball in the neck and wash purifiers before the condensers to partially cool the vapours and thus remove the heavier volatiles. The wash purifier was invented by John Grant in around 1850 and, together with the tall swan-necked stills, has the effect of producing a very light, delicate spirit.

The stills were directly heated by coal fires until 1996, and rummagers were used to remove burnt solids and burnish the interiors, thereby increasing the exposure of the low wines to copper and enhancing the flavour of the spirit. The present 10 years old malt was produced before the distillery converted to steam heating in 1996, and it will be interesting to see whether this significantly changes the flavour of the whisky.

Glen Grant malt whiskies are well known throughout the world, being among the first to be sold internationally as single malts. The "Two Highlanders" label, which was first registered in 1888, is instantly recognisable. The bulk of Glen Grant's production of 6 million litres a year is sold in Italy where it is the market

leader; although it carries no age statement, it is matured in American ex-bourbon oak casks for 5 years. The profiled malt is Glen Grant 10 years old, which is matured in a mixture of bourbon and sherry casks. Some older Glen Grant malts are available from independent bottlers.

The visitor centre includes an exhibition with a short film and there is also a shop. Visitors can sample Glen Grant's two malt whiskies in Major Grant's Study (see below left) or in the Dram Hut near the top of the garden (see left), if the weather is fine.

Feature	Profile
●	Body
● ●	Sweetness
	Smoky
	Medicinal
	Tobacco
●	Honey
	Spicy
●	Winey
● ●	Nutty
●	Malty
● ●	Fruity
●	Floral

Age 10 years
Strength 40%
Nose Light, fragrant, slightly honeyed and floral with a hint of sherry
Taste Clean, slightly sweet with a nutty, fruity flavour reminiscent of apples and pears
Cluster D Light, medium-sweet, low or no peat, with fruity, floral, malty notes and nutty hints
Similar to Glengoyne, Mannochmore, Aultmore

GLEN KEITH

{*glen*-KEITH}

The attractive buildings at Glen Keith distillery were constructed from a former meal mill using local schist stone.

Glen Keith distillery was built in 1959 beside the Linn of Keith, a beautiful waterfall at the foot of the ruins of Milton Castle. It is a most attractive distillery, rebuilt from a former mill using local stone. The waterfall feeds into a deep pool in the River Isla where wild salmon leap and swim, hence the emblem on the label depicts a salmon leaping above the Linn pool.

It draws its water from springs on Balloch Hill, and uses lightly peated malted barley. Originally designed for triple distillation with 3 stills, it was converted to double distillation in 1970 and extended to 6 stills working in pairs. The first gas-fired stills were installed here in 1957 and it pioneered the use of computers to control the whole production process, from milling to distillation.

Glen Keith Single Highland Malt whisky is available at 10 years old (profiled) in Chivas Heritage Selection. It is also used in blends such as Chivas Regal and 100 Pipers. The distillery does not have a visitor centre, or offer tours.

Feature	Profile
●●	Body
●●●	Sweetness
●	Smoky
	Medicinal
	Tobacco
●	Honey
●●	Spicy
●	Winey
●●	Nutty
●	Malty
●●	Fruity
●	Floral

Age 10 years
Strength 43%
Nose Fragrant, spicy and oaky, with a whiff of smoke
Taste Medium-sweet, nutty and fruity, with hints of ginger spice and sherry
Cluster F Medium-bodied, medium-sweet, low peat, malty notes and sherry, honey, spicy hints
Similar to Auchroisk, Tullibardine, Glenrothes

GLENKINCHIE

{*glen*-KIN-*chee*}

Established in 1837 by farmers John and George Rate, Glenkinchie Distillery was rebuilt in the 1890s, and is a fine example of a Victorian distillery incorporating listed maltings. Its name "Kinchie" is derived from the "de Quincey" family who originally owned the land and burn.

The distillery lies to the south-east of Edinburgh, in the picturesque "Garden of Scotland", perfect for growing barley and described by Robert Burns as "the most glorious corn country I have ever seen". The eighteenth-century Agricultural Revolution brought barley to East Lothian, often grown on land that had been enriched with local seaweed from the Firth of Forth. The barley ripened early and was prized for its lightness. The draff from the distillery was used to feed the local prize-winning cattle. Glenkinchie is one of only three distilleries officially classified as Lowland, the others being Auchentoshan and Bladnoch.

Glenkinchie's unusually hard water is drawn through limestone from the Lammermuir Hills and rises in a well beneath one of the warehouses. In 1981 the still house was rebuilt and converted to steam heating. The distillery uses 6 traditional wooden washbacks, 2 made from Oregon pine and 4 of Canadian larch. The copper wash still is one of the largest in the industry, distilling 20,500 litres (37,000 pints) per cycle. A cast-iron worm tub is used in preference to more modern condensers, producing a whisky of great character and depth, which has long been prized by blenders. The spirit is matured in oak casks for 10 years.

Described as "The Edinburgh Malt", Glenkinchie Lowland Scotch whisky is available at 10 years old (profiled) in Guiness UDV's Classic Malts range. It is also available in limited editions, such as a 1986 Distillers Edition finished in Amontillado casks and Glenkinchie Cask Strength (59%) numbered bottles.

The visitor centre includes an exhibition, museum and model distillery built in 1924 for the Empire Exhibition by Basset-Lowke, famed for his model steam engines. The centre and shop are open all year.

Feature	Profile
●	Body
● ●	Sweetness
●	Smoky
	Medicinal
	Tobacco
●	Honey
● ●	Spicy
	Winey
	Nutty
● ●	Malty
● ●	Fruity
● ●	Floral

Age 10 years
Strength 43%
Nose Light, sweet nose with barley-malt, green grass and a curl of smoke
Taste Fresh, light and slightly sweet showing spices, autumn fruits and harvest flavours, with hints of honey and peat
Cluster E Light, medium-sweet, low peat, with floral, malty notes and fruity, spicy, honey hints
Similar to Glenlossie, Glenallachie, Inchgower

GLENLIVET

{*glen*-LIVV-*itt*}

Glenlivet distillery was founded by George Smith, a crofter who had been distilling whisky at his farm at Upper Drumin. Following the 1823 Act of Parliament to legalize distilling, he obtained a licence in 1824, despite the opposition of the glen's illicit whisky-makers and smugglers, who threatened to burn down Smith's farm and murder him for his treachery. During these early, turbulent years Smith always carried pistols in his belt.

As his whisky became famous, it became necessary to build a larger distillery and, in 1859, Smith opened the present Glenlivet Distillery with his son John Gordon Smith. "The Glenlivet" was registered as a trademark in 1875 and is now widely recognised throughout the world as a quality single malt whisky. Glenlivet claims to be the first licensed distillery of unblended malt whisky in Scotland, and its single malt is currently America's bestseller.

Glenlivet has 8 gas-fired pot stills. Lightly-peated malt is supplied by a commercial maltings to order, and cold, soft water is drawn from a spring called Josie's Well. Although the distillery has expanded its capacity quite considerably in recent years, the mash tun, 8 Oregon pine washbacks and 8 copper stills remain virtually unaltered since the nineteenth century. A proportion of sherry casks are used for maturation, but the sherry does not dominate the final malt. In addition to the popular 12 years old (profiled), Glenlivet single malt is also available at 18 years old, at 21 years old as "The Glenlivet Archive", and in a French Limousin oak finish aged 12 years. Several vintages are also available in the Cellar Collection, including an exclusive American Oak finish.

Glenlivet Distillery is located near where the rivers Livet and Avon meet and flow onwards into the Spey, about 10 miles north of Tomintoul. The Glenlivet Reception Centre is constructed from part of the old maltings, built in 1859. It includes an exhibition of old tools used in malting,

peat cutting, distilling and cooperage. George Smith's original hair-trigger pistols are also displayed.

The visitor centre and gift shop are open from April to October, and visitors can watch the audio-visual presentation "The Ballad of the Glenlivet", take a guided tour of the distillery and sample the whiskies afterwards. There is also a coffee shop, a restaurant and a shop, and accommodation is available in Minmore house, the original nineteenth-century home of George Smith and his family.

Feature	Profile
●●	Body
●●●	Sweetness
●	Smoky
	Medicinal
	Tobacco
●●	Honey
●●	Spicy
●●	Winey
●	Nutty
●●	Malty
●●	Fruity
●●●	Floral

Age 12 years
Strength 40%
Nose Flowery, honeyed and soft
Taste Medium-bodied, quite sweet, with fruit, flowers and vanilla evident and hints of sherry and smoke
Cluster C Medium-bodied, medium-sweet, with fruity, floral, honey, malty notes and spicy hints
Similar to Glen Elgin, Glen Ord, Glendullan

GLENLOSSIE

{*glen*-LOSSY}

Glenlossie distillery was built in 1876 by John Duff, a publican and former manager of Glendronach distillery. He designed it on a slope to take advantage of gravity and used the 70 foot drop from the large dam to power a water wheel, "thereby rendering it independent of steam power". The distillery was reconstructed in 1896, when a private railway siding was added, and further improvements were made over the years until production ceased in 1917 to conserve barley stocks during World War I. It was again extended in 1962, and converted from coal-fired to steam heating in 1972.

With the exception of the fine stone still house, the buildings were constructed from cement, using sand and gravel from the River Lossie. They have very clean, white lines and classic slate roofs, and there is a single pagoda-topped malt house. A special feature is a fire engine, purpose-built in 1862 and last used when the distillery was badly damaged by fire in 1929.

Glenlossie draws its process water from the Bardon Burn, and cooling water from the Gedloch and Foths Burns. It operates a stainless steel mash tun, 4 stainless steel washbacks and 6 tall stills. Each of the spirit stills has a purifier incorporated between the lyne arm and the condenser to remove the heavier alcohols, thereby producing a lighter spirit.

The label on the bottle features a long-eared owl as its emblem, owing to the presence of owls in the woods nearby.

Glenlossie Single Malt is available at 10 years old (profiled) in Guinness UDV's Flora and Fauna range, and from some independents. It is used in Haig and Dimple blends, which account for the bulk of the production.

Glenlossie Distillery does not have a visitor centre or offer tours.

Feature	Profile
●	Body
●●	Sweetness
●	Smoky
	Medicinal
	Tobacco
●	Honey
●●	Spicy
	Winey
●	Nutty
●●	Malty
●●	Fruity
●●	Floral

Age 10 years
Strength 43%
Nose Light fresh aroma, with grassy, floral notes
Taste Medium-sweet with malt and spice notes, and a hint of smoke
Cluster E Light, medium-sweet, low peat, with floral, malty notes and fruity, spicy, honey hints
Similar to Glenkinchie, Glenallachie, Loch Lomond

SPEYSIDE
SINGLE MALT SCOTCH WHISKY

The three *spirit stills* at the

GLENLOSSIE

distillery have *purifiers* installed between the *lyne arm* and the condenser. This has a bearing on the *character* of the single MALT SCOTCH WHISKY produced which has a *fresh*, grassy aroma and a *smooth*, lingering flavour. Built in 1876 by *John Duff* the distillery lies four miles *south* of ELGIN in *Morayshire*

A G E D **10** Y E A R S

GLENMORANGIE

{glen-MOR-angie}

Glenmorangie is Gaelic for "glen of tranquillity". Situated at Tain in the north of Scotland, overlooking the Dornoch Firth, it was founded by William Mathieson in 1849. The adverts emphasize the tranquil setting in which Glenmorangie malt whiskies are patiently crafted by the "sixteen men of Tain", thus securing their lifetime employment.

The distillery has 8 swan-necked stills, the tallest in Scotland at nearly 17 feet, and it is claimed that these elegant stills produce a lighter, purer spirit. Its water, unusually hard and rich in minerals, is drawn through sandstone from Tarlogie Springs. The whisky is matured in bourbon barrels, made from American mountain oaks at least a 100 years old and grown on the north-facing slopes of the Ozark mountains of Missouri. The whiskies are bottled from a

combination of first and second fill barrels of at least 10 years' maturation.

Glenmorangie Single Highland Malt at 10 years old (profiled) is Scotland's best-selling malt whisky, it is also the second best seller in the UK and third in the world. It is also available at 15 years old and 18 years old, and in three special wood finishes -port, sherry and madeira. This new range was introduced in 1995 and, in 1999, a limited fino sherry wood finish was added. Glenmorangie was the first distillery to introduce special wood finishes other than sherry, a trend that has since been widely copied.

Glenmorangie also offers several special editions, such as a 1977 vintage, Special Reserve, Elegance, Millennium Malt, Manager's Choisce, Original Malt, Cellar 13 and Traditional.

Glenmorangie distillery is open all year to visitors for tours and tastings. There is a visitor centre in a converted still house, with a working steam engine and a model still. Virtual tours are available on the Glenmorangie website.

Feature	Profile
●●	Body
●●	Sweetness
●	Smoky
●	Medicinal
	Tobacco
●	Honey
●●	Spicy
	Winey
●●	Nutty
●	Malty
●●	Fruity
●●	Floral

Age 10 years
Strength 40%
Nose Vanilla, citrus and butterscotch
Taste Creamy, soft and fresh with fruit, flowers, spice and nutty flavours
Cluster H Medium-bodied, medium-sweet, with smoky, fruity, spicy notes and floral, nutty hints
Similar to Balblair, Craigellachie, Teaninich

GLEN MORAY

{*glen*-MURRAY}

Glen Moray distillery nestles between the River Lossie and Gallow Hill on the outskirts of Elgin, Speyside's historic capital. As the name suggests, Gallow Hill is where the convicted criminals of Elgin were hanged, and human remains from unmarked graves have indeed been uncovered here during excavations. Although the last hanging was in 1697, there is still a brooding eeriness to this spot, with suitable orchestration provided by the resident rooks as they circle and dive from their nests in the rustling pines on the hill.

Founded in 1815 as a brewery, Glen Moray was converted to a distillery in 1897 and has now been producing whisky for over a century. Its water is drawn from a well beside the River Lossie, and it operates a stainless steel mash tun, 5 stainless steel washbacks and 4 copper pot stills. The whisky is matured in ex-bourbon American oak casks, then finished for 6 months in Chardonnay and Chenin Blanc casks that have been specially selected from the Loire region of France.

The recent success of Glen Moray as a single malt is largely due to a happy accident in the 1990s, when it was discovered that a white wine finish greatly enhanced the light, floral character of the whisky. "Are we talking white wine or single malt?" hints Glen Moray's advert suggestively. There is no doubt that it is whisky, but finishing in wine casks adds a very attractive lighter dimension to its flavour that appeals to wine drinkers.

Until fairly recently, most of Glen Moray's production went for blending, but the new white wine expressions are becoming increasingly popular as single malts of distinction in their own right. Glen Moray is available as a malt bearing no age statement, at 12 years old (profiled), at 16 years old, and in special bottlings such as a centenary malt with a Port finish and a Manager's Special 1981 matured in a sherry cask and not chill-filtered.

Glen Moray distillery and gift shop are open to visitors all year. Guided tours by distillery workers are available, giving visitors the opportunity to learn first-hand the secrets of their historic craft.

Feature	Profile
●	Body
● ●	Sweetness
●	Smoky
	Medicinal
	Tobacco
●	Honey
● ●	Spicy
●	Winey
● ●	Nutty
● ●	Malty
● ●	Fruity
● ● ● ●	Floral

Age 12 years
Strength 40%
Nose Fruity and creamy with vanilla, citrus and heather notes
Taste Nutty and spicy, with fruit, floral and menthol flavours and a whiff of peat
Cluster E Light, medium-sweet, low peat, with floral, malty notes and fruity, spicy, honey hints
Similar to Bunnahabhain, Glenlossie, Glenallachie

GLEN ORD

{*glen*-ORD}

Just north of Inverness, on Eilean Dubh – the legendary "Black Isle" – can be found Glen Ord Distillery. It was first licensed for whisky production in 1838 by Robert Johnstone and Donald McLennan, but records of an alehouse and meal mill date from 1549. Indeed it was John Mackenzie's sixteenth-century meal mill that provided the focus of village life at Muir of Ord for four centuries, where local farmers would bring their oats and barley to be milled. The modernized replacement, Ord Maltings, now supplies malted barley to several other distilleries in north-west Scotland, using a combination of local peat and oil-fired kilns.

Glen Ord Distillery was extensively modified and refurbished in 1896, when it ranked as one of the top distilleries in Scotland. At the start of the twentieth century Glen Ord was a major producer with a workforce of around 100 men. Sturdy Clydesdale horses and carts transported milled meal and whisky to

the railway station at Muir of Ord, returning with fresh barley for the maltings – it was not unknown for the carter to be "the worse o' wear", relying on his horse to find its way back to the maltings. The distillery was lit by paraffin lamps until 1939 when electricity was first connected.

Glen Ord is the last of 9 distilleries that operated around Muir of Ord in the nineteenth century. The rich agricultural land of the Black Isle produces fine barley, and offers an ideal location for whisky production with its plentiful supply of peat on the moor, and continuous pure peaty water flowing from Loch nan Eun and Loch nan Bonnach into Allt Fionnaidh (the "white burn").

Until recently, Glen Ord whisky was mostly used for blending; but in the 1990s, the 12 years old single malt (profiled) was re-launched with immediate success, winning several international awards. Not that exporting is a new venture at Glen Ord – in its nineteenth-century heyday, Alfred Barnard recorded that the whisky was shipped to "Singapore, South Africa and other colonies". Glen Ord is also available in Guinness UDV's Rare Malts series at 23 years old (60.8%).

The distillery's visitor centre, a converted warehouse, is open all year, offering tours and whisky tastings. It includes an attractive exhibition on the history of the distillery and the Black Isle. Visitors can purchase a range of whiskies and other goods in the distillery shop.

Feature	Profile
●●●	Body
●●	Sweetness
●	Smoky
	Medicinal
	Tobacco
●	Honey
●●	Spicy
●	Winey
●	Nutty
●●	Malty
●●	Fruity
●●	Floral

Age 12 years
Strength 40%
Nose Malty, sweet and a hint of smoke
Taste Medium-bodied, spicy fruit and floral flavour, with honey and sherry notes and a long finish
Cluster C Medium-bodied, medium-sweet, with fruity, floral, honey, malty notes and spicy hints
Similar to Glendullan, Glenlivet, Balvenie

GLENROTHES

*{glen-*ROTH-*is}*

The Glen of Dounie at the fringe of Rothes is the pretty location for Glenrothes distillery, which lies on the banks of the peaty burn of Rothes and is flanked by the ancient village graveyard. The distillery draws its water from Ardcanny Spring, known locally as "The Lady's Well" after the only daughter of the fourteenth-century Earl of Rothes. Legend has it that she was murdered beside the spring by the "Wolf of Badenoch" while trying to protect her lover.

Fine malt whisky has been distilled here since Glenrothes first opened in 1879. The distillery was extended in 1896, but a fire on 15th May 1922 caused many casks to explode and large quantities of matured whisky poured into the burn. It is said that the locals enjoyed a free toddy from the burn that day, scooping it up in pots, pans and even their boots. An angler claimed that the trout, unusually docile from the whisky in the water, were easily caught!

Glenrothes Distillery was fully modernized in 1980 and produces 1.6 million litres per annum. It operates a large, stainless steel mash tun producing 4 tonnes of mash per cycle, 12 Oregon pine washbacks, 5 low wines stills and 5 spirit stills. Fermentation lasts about two days, and only cultured yeast is used. The spirit stills are unusually larger than the low wines stills, with the result that Glenrothes produces a heavier spirit than other Speyside distilleries. The whole process, including distillation, is controlled automatically from the still room by a sophisticated computer system. The lightly-peated malt used at the distillery is supplied to order from Tamdhu Maltings, and the whisky is matured in a mixture of Spanish and American oak casks, prepared with both sherry and bourbon.

Limited quantities of the best casks are individually selected from a given year's distillation, when judged to be at the peak of their perfection, and bottled as the Glenrothes Vintage Malt for that year. Not all the casks from one year necessarily meet the Master Blender's high quality criteria and, therefore, a "vintage" is not produced every year. Each bottle carries the date of distillation and year of bottling – the profiled malt was distilled in 1989, bottled in 2000, and hence matured for 11 years.

Glenrothes is sold in a clear glass bottle that reflects the style of sample bottles typically found in a blending room. This understated bottle emphasizes the quality of the whisky, which is highly prized by many Master Blenders. The bulk of the production goes for blending, and Glenrothes is the signature malt in Cutty Sark Scots Whisky, a premium blend sold worldwide by Cutty Sark International. Glenrothes is also available from Gordon & MacPhail at 8 years old (the MacPhail's Collection) and separately as a vintage. Glenrothes distillery is not open to the public.

Feature	Profile
●●	Body
●●●	Sweetness
●	Smoky
	Medicinal
	Tobacco
●	Honey
●	Spicy
●●	Winey
●	Nutty
●●	Malty
●●	Fruity
	Floral

Age 12 years
Strength 43%
Nose Rich, sweet and honeyed, with sherry, vanilla and malt evident
Taste Medium-smooth body, light smoke, multi-layered with hints of fruit, vanilla and spice, and a long finish
Cluster F Medium-bodied, medium-sweet, low peat, malty notes and sherry, honey, spicy hints
Similar to Auchroisk, Glen Keith, Deanston

GLEN SCOTIA

{glen-SCO-sha}

In the ancient town of Campbeltown, the Celtic lord Dalruadhain crowned Scotland's early kings on the Stone of Destiny. At the end of the eighteenth century there were at least 34 illicit stills operating here, and Glen Scotia distillery was probably one of them, although it was not licensed until 1835. By 1887, Campbeltown had 21 licensed distillers, producing 10 million litres of whisky a year and employing over 250 men. In the 1960s it featured in a minor hit record by the singer Andie Stewart, with the memorable line "Oh Campbeltown Loch I wish you were whisky, I would drink you dry".

Campbeltown has long enjoyed a reputation as the "cradle" of Scotch whisky – in 1887, Alfred Barnard described it as "whisky city". It is the only town to have been listed as a whisky region. It was used as a source by bootleggers during American prohibition, but the quality of its whisky declined and most of the producers ceased operating. Sadly, only two distilleries now operate in Campbeltown – Springbank and Glen Scotia.

Glen Scotia operates a small distillery that could easily be mistaken for a Victorian townhouse. It has its own resident ghost, a previous owner Duncan MacCallum who drowned himself in Campbeltown Loch and returns to haunt the night shift. The distillery was reconstructed in 1894 and substantially upgraded in 1992. Following a further period of silence, it resumed production in 1999.

Its water is drawn from two deep wells below the distillery and from Crosshill Loch and it uses moderately peated malted barley. It operates a steel mash tun, 6 steel wash backs and 2 swan-necked stills. The whisky is matured in a mixture of American bourbon oak, European sherry casks, and some refills racked 9 high in a modern warehouse at the distillery.

Glen Scotia Single Malt whisky is available at 14 years old (profiled), and

at 8 years old. It is quite typical of the briny, peaty malt whiskies formerly produced in Campbeltown. We look forward to the new whiskies becoming available at the end of the decade.

Glen Scotia distillery does not have a visitor centre but offers tours in summer, by appointment, and has a small shop.

Feature	Profile
●●	Body
●●	Sweetness
●●	Smoky
●●	Medicinal
	Tobacco
●	Honey
	Spicy
●	Winey
●●	Nutty
●●	Malty
●	Fruity
●	Floral

Age 14 years
Strength 40%
Nose Lightly perfumed, malty and peaty notes, with a salty tang
Taste Medium-bodied, not too sweet, spirity with nutty, honey notes and light fruit
Cluster I Medium-light, dry, with smoky, spicy, honey notes and nutty, floral hints
Similar to Highland Park, Springbank, Isle of Jura

GLEN SPEY

{*glen*-SPEY}

Glen Spey distillery was built at Rothes in 1885 by James Stuart, who also owned Macallan until 1892. It was originally an extension to the Mill of Rothes, and retains pleasant Victorian buildings, though it was rebuilt in 1969 when extended to 4 stills. It stands below the ruins of Castle Rothes, the home of the Earls of Rothes since the fourteenth century. Castle Rothes was unfortunately burnt down by locals in 1620 to prevent it becoming a refuge for thieves.

It draws its water from the Doonie Burn and uses lightly peated malted barley. It operates a semi-Lauter mash tun, 8 stainless steel washbacks and 4 stills. In fact, Glen Spey was the first to install this type of mash tun. The whisky is matured in ex-bourbon and refill casks, stored in traditional warehouses at the distillery. The emblem on the label is the Goldcrest, Britain's smallest bird, which can be heard warbling in the Scots pines beside Castle Rothes.

Glen Spey Single Highland Malt whisky is available at 12 years old

(profiled), at 8 years old bottled under the previous management of Justerini and Brooks, and from some independents. The bulk of the production goes for blending, and it is used principally in Guinness UDV's J&B blend and in Spey Royal.

Glen Spey distillery does not have a visitor centre or offer tours.

Feature	Profile
●	Body
●●●	Sweetness
●	Smoky
	Medicinal
	Tobacco
	Honey
●	Spicy
●	Winey
●	Nutty
●●	Malty
	Fruity
●●	Floral

Age 12 years
Strength 40%
Nose Aromatic, malty and floral
Taste Light and sweet, with a malty, floral character and hints of peat smoke, sherry and spice
Cluster G Medium-bodied, sweet, low peat and floral notes
Similar to Glenfiddich, Miltonduff, Dufftown

SPEYSIDE
SINGLE MALT
SCOTCH WHISKY

The Scots Pines beside *the ruins of*
ROTHES CASTLE, provide an *ideal habitat*
for the *GOLDCREST*, *Britain's smallest bird*,
and overlook the

GLEN SPEY

distillery. Founded in 1885, *the distillery was*
originally part of the *Mills of Rothes*. Water
from the DOONIE BURN is used to produce
this *smooth, warming single MALT SCOTCH*
WHISKY. A slight sense of *wood smoke on*
the nose is rewarded with a *spicy, dry* finish.

AGED 12 YEARS

43% vol   70cl

GLENTURRET

{*glen*-TURRET}

Built in 1775 and licensed in 1826, Glenturret claims to be Scotland's oldest distillery. Despite being one of the smallest distilleries in Scotland, it is also the most visited, offering fine hospitality to 200,000 visitors a year. The reasons for its popularity include its central location: only an hour from Glasgow and Edinburgh, its picturesque setting and its excellent facilities.

Nestling beside the Turret Burn, near Crieff in Perthshire, Glenturret is a traditional distillery, malting its own barley and distilling its whiskies in relatively small quantities using pot stills. Its most famous resident was Towser, whose 24 years of duty as distillery cat are commemorated by a bronze statue and an entry in the Guinness Book of Records.

Glenturret Single Highland Malt is available at 12 years old (profiled), and at 8, 15, 18, 21 and 25 years old. A cask-strength 10 years old (57.1%) is also produced, as are two malt liqueurs. It is also available in special editions, including a ceramic flagon and globe, and through independents such as MacPhail's Collection, Murray McDavid and Signatory. Glenturret whiskies are well balanced and have won many awards.

Visitors are welcome at Glenturret Distillery all year round. It has an excellent visitor centre with a "Water of Life" audio-visual presentation and a "Spirit of the Glen" exhibition. As well as a guided tour, there is a chance to sample the full range of Glenturret Single Highland Malts in the Whisky Tasting Bar, or browse in the gift shop.

Glenturret has extensive catering facilities, including the Smugglers Restaurant (a converted whisky warehouse), the Pagoda Room and the Kiln Room, where visitors can enjoy anything from morning coffee to a three-course meal. The most recent addition is a fine conference suite, with modern audio-visual facilities and flexible lecture accommodation. Evening functions, such as Burns' night suppers and *ceilidhs*, are also available for which advance booking is essential.

Feature	Profile
●●	Body
●●●	Sweetness
●	Smoky
	Medicinal
	Tobacco
●●	Honey
●●	Spicy
●●	Winey
●●	Nutty
●●	Malty
●	Fruity
●●	Floral

Age 12 years
Strength 40%
Nose Floral, malty and peppery, with a whiff of smoke
Taste Light, medium-sweet, well-balanced with nutty, malty notes and hints of honey, vanilla and spices
Cluster B Medium-bodied, medium-sweet, with nutty, malty, floral, honey and fruity notes
Similar to Knockando, Aberfeldy, Blair Athol

HIGHLAND PARK

{*high-land*-PARK}

Situated on the island of Orkney to the west of Kirkwall, Highland Park is the most northerly distillery in the world. It was founded by Magnus Eunson in the late eighteenth century, one of many Orcadian smugglers and illicit whisky producers who rebelled against the heavy excise duties imposed to help finance the war with France. It is said that he used his position as church officer to conceal whisky beneath the church pulpit and in coffins! The distillery was licensed in 1826 by Robert Borwick whose son-in-law, the local Exciseman John Robertson, is generally credited with routing out the smugglers. It was no coincidence that Robertson had acquired the distillery and surrounding land from Magnus Eunson prior to Borwick commencing legal production.

Highland Park is one of the few distilleries to use hard water, and its supply is drawn from Cattie Maggie's Springs. Also unusual is the use of a traditional malting floor for germinating the barley, which is then dried over a fire of local aromatic heather peat, cut from nearby Hobbister Moor. This is the source of the heathery smokiness that is characteristic of Highland Park whiskies, which are nowadays lightened by adding some unpeated mainland malted barley.

In addition to the 12 years old (profiled) Highland Park is also available at 18 years old, at 25 years old and in special vintage bottlings. The whisky is matured in a mixture of ex-bourbon and sherry casks that impart slightly sherried, honeyed and malty flavours. The overall result is a medium-bodied, multi-layered, complex malt

whisky with peat smoke evident, but by no means dominant, and heather, honey and malty notes also present.

Highland Park's visitor centre and shop are open on weekdays all year, and also at weekends during the summer. The tour includes a new audio-visual presentation about the history of the distillery and its production methods and visitors have the opportunity to taste the whiskies.

Feature	Profile
●●	Body
●●	Sweetness
●●●	Smoky
●	Medicinal
	Tobacco
●●	Honey
●	Spicy
●	Winey
●	Nutty
●●	Malty
●	Fruity
●	Floral

Age 12 years
Strength 40%
Nose Heather-honey sweetness and peaty smokiness
Taste Smoky sweetness layered with heather, malt and honey notes
Cluster I Medium-light, dry, with smoky, spicy, honey notes and nutty, floral hints
Similar to Bowmore, Springbank, Bruichladdich

INCHGOWER

{*inch*-GOW-*er*}

Inchgower distillery was built by Alexander Wilson in 1871, outside the fishing village of Buckie. Its origins can be traced to Tochieneal distillery, established in 1824 on the estate of the Earl of Seafield. It is an attractive distillery with a pretty courtyard, formerly flanked by a carpenter's shop, cooperage, blacksmith and workers' cottages, and has a stone still house and twin pagoda-topped chimneys. Until the early twentieth century, the adjoining farm reared cattle, sheep and pigs on the by-products from the distillery, including champion Aberdeen Angus bulls.

The emblem on the bottle is the oyster catcher, and examples of

these birds can be seen on the sands beyond Buckie.

Inchgower's process water is drawn from springs in the Menduff hills, and cooling water is supplied by Buckie Burn. It operates a stainless steel mash tun, 6 Oregon pine washbacks and 4 stills. The whisky is matured in ex-bourbon American oak casks.

Inchgower Single Malt is available at 14 years old (profiled) in Guinness UDV's Flora and Fauna range, at 22 years old as a cask-strength malt (55.7%) in the Rare Malts series, and from some independents. It is used in Bell's blends, which account for most of its production.

Inchgower does not have a visitor centre or offer tours.

Feature	Profile
●	Body
●●●	Sweetness
●	Smoky
●	Medicinal
	Tobacco
●●	Honey
●●	Spicy
	Winey
●	Nutty
●●	Malty
●	Fruity
●●	Floral

Age 14 years
Strength 43%
Nose Aromatic sweetness, malty and honeyed
Taste Fruity, spicy, and oaky notes, with hints of seaside and smoke
Cluster E Light, medium-sweet, low peat, with floral, malty notes and fruity, spicy, honey hints
Similar to Tomintoul, Glenallachie, Glenlossie

SPEYSIDE
SINGLE MALT
SCOTCH WHISKY

The *Oyster Catcher* is a common sight around the

INCHGOWER

distillery, which stands *close* to the *sea*, on the mouth of the *RIVER SPEY* near *BUCKIE*. *Inchgower*, established in 1824, produces *one* of the most *distinctive single* malt whiskies in *SPEYSIDE*. It is a malt for the *discerning drinker* ~ a complex aroma precedes a *fruity, spicy* taste with a hint of *salt*.

AGED **14** YEARS

43% vol   70cl

ISLE OF JURA

*{isle-o'-*JEW*-ra}*

It is estimated that the red deer of the Hebridean island of Jura outnumber the human residents by about thirty to one. Indeed, the name Jura is Norse for "deer island". Nestling at Craighouse, in the shadow of the Paps of Jura which tower 2,500 feet (762 m) above, lies the distillery. Due to the Gulf Stream, the climate is mild, and palm trees flourish. To get there, take the Feolin Ferry from Islay and follow the road – there is only one, and it leads directly to the distillery. George Orwell once took this road, and wrote his famous novel *1984* here.

Alfred Barnard visited the distillery in 1887, fell in love with it, and wrote about its workings and beautiful setting. Then, Jura's population was about 1,000 – today it is less than a quarter of that.

Using lightly-peated malt, the distillery produces a light, dry whisky that is not typical of other island malts, and provides Jura's only industry after farming and fishing. It is claimed that whisky has been distilled here since 1502. The present distillery was established in 1810. After a period of closure from 1918–60, it was rebuilt in 1960 and extended in the 1970s to 4 large stills that are more like a Highland distillery than those of its neighbours on Islay.

The distillery uses the crystal-clear water drawn from the Bhaile Mhargaidh Spring, which means the "Market Loch" in Gaelic. In addition to the popular 10 years old Isle of Jura Highland malt (profiled), the distillery also bottles malts at 16 years old, 21 years old and, occasionally, at 26 and 36 years old.

The distillery has a visitor centre, and tours can be arranged by appointment.

Feature	Profile
●●	Body
●	Sweetness
●●	Smoky
●●	Medicinal
	Tobacco
●	Honey
●	Spicy
	Winey
●●	Nutty
●	Malty
●	Fruity
●	Floral

Age 10 years
Strength 40%
Nose Aromatic, somewhat dry and smoky
Taste Salty and oily, with nutty and peaty notes and the suggestion of heather, almonds and pine
Cluster I Medium-light, dry, with smoky, spicy, honey notes and nutty, floral hints
Similar to Bruichladdich, Springbank, Glen Scotia

KNOCKANDO

{knock-AN-do}

Knockando, in Gaelic "Cnoc-an-dhu", means the "little black hill". The distillery lies on a steep wooded bank of the River Spey, and draws its water exclusively from the Cardnach Spring. It is claimed that the special purity of this water determines the unique character of Knockando malt whiskies. Bonnie Prince Charlie's army camped here on the banks of the Spey in 1745, on their way to the fateful battle of Culloden. Several of the buildings still retain a Victorian charm, including the former station of Knockando which is now used as a trade centre. The distillery was established in 1898, and extended in 1969. It uses very lightly peated barley, and operates a stainless steel mash tun, 8 Oregon pine washbacks and 4 stills.

The malt whiskies produced at Knockando are all distilled in a particular year, or "season". A few sherry casks are used for maturation, along with ex-bourbon and refills, imparting a subtle sherry influence and body. The profiled vintage is of the 12 years old Knockando distilled in 1987 and bottled in 1999 at 40%. Other vintages are aged for longer, or bottled at 43%, and can be drier. Much of the production goes for J&B blending, but the Knockando single malt can be obtained through specialist whisky retailers and in markets.

Knockando does not have a visitor centre, though tours of the distillery are possible by appointment.

Feature	Profile
●●	Body
●●●	Sweetness
●	Smoky
	Medicinal
	Tobacco
●●	Honey
●●	Spicy
●	Winey
●●	Nutty
●	Malty
●●	Fruity
●●	Floral

Age 12 years
Strength 40%
Nose Floral, sweet and honeyed
Taste Medium-bodied, subtle flavour with grass, nuts and spice showing, and hints of sherry and peat
Cluster B Medium-bodied, medium-sweet, with nutty, malty, floral, honey and fruity notes
Similar to Glenturret, Benromach, Scapa

LAGAVULIN

*{laga-*VOO-*lin}*

Lagavulin is Gaelic for "the hollow where the mill is". Nestling on the southern coast of Islay, near the brooding ruin of Dunyvaig Castle, it is one of the oldest distilleries in Scotland. In the twelfth century Dunyvaig was occupied by Somerled, the first Lord of the Isles, who is credited with driving the Vikings from the west of Scotland. Hence Lagavulin's distinctive, complex malt is styled "Lord of the Isles – the definitive Islay malt". The distillery's sharp lines and white buildings, with their twin pagoda-topped chimneys, date from Victorian times and contrast starkly against the rugged foreshore and heather-clad hills beyond.

Whisky has been produced here since the early eighteenth century, with ten stills thought to have been operating in the 1740s. Lagavulin distillery was first licensed in 1816 to John Johnston. It was acquired by White Horse Distillers in 1924, and is now part of Guinness UDV's portfolio.

The distillery's water is drawn from Solan Lochs, having passed through heavy peat bogs which, together with the heavily-peated malted barley, contributes to its distinctively pungent character. The barley is malted to order at Port Ellen Maltings, having been dried over a fire of peat cut from a local moss. The distillery operates a large stainless steel mash tun, 10 larch washbacks, and 4 squat onion-shaped stills with swan-necked lyne pipes. The whisky is matured in ex-bourbon American oak casks, combined with a few sherry casks for finishing. The casks are stored in the maturation sheds above the beach – it's no surprise, therefore, that the whisky carries a strong whiff of seaweed and fresh, salty Atlantic air.

Lagavulin single malt whisky was being supplied to the colonies as early as 1875, but most went for blending until the 1980s when it was launched as one of Guinness UDV's Classic Malts.

Lagavulin 16 years old (profiled) is now their best seller, with demand far outstripping the supply, and it has won several gold medals in recent international competitions. Lagavulin also regularly produces special editions, such as a double-matured 1981 Distiller's Edition using Pedro Jiminez Sherry casks for the final finish.

Lagavulin distillery has a shop, offers tours and tastings and welcomes visitors on weekdays all year round.

Feature	Profile
●●●●	Body
●	Sweetness
●●●●	Smoky
●●●●	Medicinal
●	Tobacco
	Honey
●	Spicy
●●	Winey
●	Nutty
●	Malty
●	Fruity
	Floral

Age 16 years
Strength 43%
Nose Powerful peat smoke with iodine and seaweed and a hint of malty sweetness
Taste Dry peat smoke and roasted chestnuts with a salty, sherried note and a complex finish
Cluster J Full-bodied, dry, pungent, peaty and medicinal, with spicy, tobacco notes
Similar to Laphroaig, Ardbeg, Clynelish

LAPHROAIG

{*la*-FROY'*g*}

Laphroaig is Gaelic for "the beautiful hollow by the broad bay" and on a sunny day it truly lives up to its name. The distillery was built in 1815 by Donald and Alex Johnston at a remote spot on the windswept southern coast of Islay. Its neat Victorian stone buildings seem almost to challenge the elements – white-washed granite walls with orderly rows of black-framed windows, twin pagoda-topped kilns, and maturation sheds that announce "LAPHROAIG" in tall bold letters that face defiantly across the Atlantic.

Laphroaig is made by first steeping the barley in soft, peaty Islay water and allowing it to germinate, which involves raking and turning it by hand on the malting floor for three days. The germinated barley is then dried in a swirling peat fire, and it's the smoke from this pungent Islay peat that gives Laphroaig its distinctive "peaty reek" character. After distillation the whisky is matured in Kentucky oak casks, racked in the maturation sheds on the seashore (to the right of the photograph). Here it is washed by the cool, salty wind from the Atlantic, and on a stormy night the sea has been

known to enter the sheds, swirling beneath the barrels. It's no surprise, therefore, that Laphroaig's unique, peaty taste also carries a strong hint of iodine and sharp, salty Atlantic air.

Like the islanders, Laphroaig is uncompromising and hardy – "you'll love it or hate it" warns the advert. It has been likened to mouthwash or disinfectant, and American doctors were allowed to prescribe it "for medicinal purposes" during prohibition. It is styled "the definitive Islay malt whisky" because it epitomises the taste of Islay – rich, smoky, peaty and full of character. It is a whisky that releases the pungent, earthy aroma of blue peat smoke, the sweet nuttiness of the barley and the delicate, heathery perfume of Islay's streams. Laphroaig is definitely an acquired taste, but it is one shared by the Prince of Wales who has commissioned his own "Highgrove" edition.

Water is drawn from Kilbride Loch, having run over heather-clad granite hills and through acres of peat bogs. The distillery operates original floor maltings and kiln, a stainless steel Lauter mash tun, 6 stainless steel washbacks, 3 wash stills, 3 small spirit stills and one larger one, to maintain the balance of the product. The whisky is matured exclusively in ex-bourbon American oak casks, in warehouses next to the sea.

Laphroaig Single Islay Malt whisky is bottled at 10 years old (profiled), at 15 years old, at 30 years old and at 10 years old cask-strength (57.3%), the latter not chill-filtered. Special editions are also produced from time to time.

The visitor centre is open all year round, offers tours and tastings, and there is a shop. For those not able to get to Islay, the website offers an excellent virtual distillery tour.

Feature	Profile
●●●●	Body
●●	Sweetness
●●●●	Smoky
●●●●	Medicinal
●	Tobacco
	Honey
	Spicy
●	Winey
●	Nutty
●	Malty
	Fruity
	Floral

Age 10 years
Strength 40%
Nose Pungent, earthy aroma of blue peat smoke
Taste Very peaty, smoky, salty and medicinal with some malt and nuttiness
Cluster J Full-bodied, dry, pungent, peaty and medicinal, with spicy, tobacco notes
Similar to Lagavulin, Ardbeg, Clynelish

LINKWOOD

{LINK-*wood*}

Linkwood distillery was built by Peter Brown in 1821 on the River Lossie, near Elgin. The original stone still house and single pagoda-topped malt house have been preserved and are still in use. When it was rebuilt by his son William Brown in 1873, the *Elgin Courant* of 1874 reported that "the aqua it produces is quite equal to that which attained the celebrity of Linkwood whisky". Great care has always been taken to maintain consistency with the original whisky, to the extent that faithful replicas of the original two stills were commissioned in 1971, complete with bumps and dents, so as to safeguard the character of the spirit.

The emblem on the label is a pair of swans, frequent residents of the Linkwood Burn above the dam that collects the cooling water. Process water is drawn from springs near Milbuies Loch. The distillery operates a cast iron copper-topped mash tun, 11 Oregon pine washbacks and 6 stills – 4 in the new extension and 2 in the original still house.

Linkwood Single Malt whisky is available at 12 years old (profiled) in Guinness UDV's Flora and Fauna range, at 23 years old as a cask-strength malt (58.4%) in the Rare Malts range, and from some independents. It is also used in blends which take the bulk of the production.

Linkwood distillery does not have a visitor centre or offer tours.

Feature	Profile
●●	Body
●●●	Sweetness
●	Smoky
	Medicinal
	Tobacco
●	Honey
●	Spicy
●●	Winey
	Nutty
●	Malty
●●●	Fruity
●●	Floral

Age 12 years
Strength 43%
Nose Fragrant and sweet, with a whiff of smoke
Taste Fruity and floral with honey, malt and spice notes
Cluster C Medium-bodied, medium-sweet, with fruity, floral, honey, malty notes and spicy hints
Similar to Glendullan, Glen Elgin, Royal Brackla

SPEYSIDE
SINGLE MALT
SCOTCH WHISKY

LINKWOOD

distillery stands on the *River Lossie*, close to *ELGIN* in *Speyside*. The *distillery* has retained its *traditional atmosphere* since its *establishment* in 1821. Great care *&* has always been taken to *safeguard* the character of the *whisky* which has remained the same through the years. Linkwood is one of the FINEST *&* Single Malt Scotch Whiskies available - *full bodied* with a hint of *sweetness* and a *slightly smoky aroma*.

YEARS **12** OLD

Distilled & Bottled in SCOTLAND.
LINKWOOD DISTILLERY
Elgin, Moray, Scotland.

43% vol   70 cl

LOCH LOMOND

{*loch*-LOW-*mond*}

As its name suggests, Loch Lomond distillery is located beside the famous loch. It is just above the "Highland Line" and as such its whisky can be described as a single Highland malt. The distillery, which is a short distance from the world famous championship Loch Lomond Golf Course, has its own cooperage, where the oak barrels used for maturation are crafted and repaired.

One of the few privately-owned distillery groups in Scotland, Loch Lomond has expanded rapidly in recent years with the addition of Glen Scotia and Littlemill Distilleries, which were closed by their previous owners. The malts from these "lost" distilleries will not come back on stream until later in the decade.

It has 4 unusual stills with rectifying heads and 2 conventional pot stills, which together can produce 8 different malt whiskies. The rectifying heads cause heavier vapours to fall back as reflux to be evaporated again, allowing only the lighter volatiles to pass into the condenser initially. When a short middle cut is taken the resulting

spirit is lighter, whereas longer runs produce a heavier spirit, and hence the character of the resulting whisky is varied.

Loch Lomond Single Highland Malt whisky is available with no age statement (profiled), and as Inchmurrin 10 years old and Old Rhosdhu 5 years old, each with different degrees of peated barley; there is also a Loch Lomond single blend. Other less well known malt whiskies called Loch Lomond HP, Glen Douglas, Craiglodge, Inchmoan, and Croftengea are produced.

Loch Lomond distillery does not have a visitor centre or offer tours.

Feature	Profile
●	Body
●	Sweetness
●	Smoky
●	Medicinal
	Tobacco
●	Honey
●	Spicy
	Winey
●	Nutty
●●	Malty
●	Fruity
●●	Floral

Age No age statement
Strength 40%
Nose Scented, minty aroma
Taste Spicy with citric and floral notes, and a hint of honeyed smoke
Cluster E Light, medium-sweet, low peat, with floral, malty notes and fruity, spicy, honey hints
Similar to Glenlossie, Bunnahabhain, Glenkinchie

LONGMORN

{*long*-MORN}

Longmorn is Gaelic for the "place of the holy man" because the distillery is on the site of an ancient chapel. It was built in 1894 by John Duff who also built its sister distillery Benriach, both of which were linked to the railway. Although Longmorn Station is no longer operating it is retained as a feature, as are a Victorian water wheel and a steam engine.

Longmorn is an attractive Victorian sandstone distillery, with a pagoda-topped chimney, that nestles below Blackhills. The emblem on its bottle is an osprey, a bird which has recently returned to the Spey forests after being hunted to the point of extinction.

Its malted barley is supplied lightly-peated to order by maltsters, and its water is drawn from the peaty burnside springs which rise in the Blackhills. It operates a stainless steel mash tun, 8 stainless steel washbacks and 8 small pot stills. The whisky is matured in a mixture of ex-bourbon American oak and European sherry casks. Production is quite high at 3.5 million litres a year, most of which goes for blending.

The stills were directly heated by coal fires until 1993, with rummagers to remove burnt solids and burnish the interiors. This increases the exposure of the low wines to copper and thus enhances the flavour of the spirit. The present 15 years old malt was produced before the distillery converted to steam heating, and it will be interesting to see whether this significantly changes the flavour of the whisky.

Longmorn Single Highland Malt whisky is available at 15 years old (profiled), at 25 years old as a "Centenary" edition (1994), and through independents. It is used in Chivas blends, such as Chivas Regal and in Seagram's Heritage Selection.

Longmorn distillery does not have a visitor centre or offer tours.

The Longmorn workforce of 1914 with an original steam engine in the background.

Feature	Profile
●●●	Body
●●	Sweetness
●	Smoky
	Medicinal
	Tobacco
●	Honey
●	Spicy
●	Winey
●●●	Nutty
●●●	Malty
●●	Fruity
●●●	Floral

Age 15 years
Strength 45%
Nose Aromatic, floral and honeyed. Some sherry and spice discernible
Taste Full-bodied, floral and fruity with malty caramel notes, a touch of sherried spice and smoke
Cluster B Medium-bodied, medium-sweet, with nutty, malty, floral, honey and fruity notes
Similar to Edradour, Strathisla, Scapa

MACALLAN

{*ma*-CALLAN}

Macallan distillery was one of the first to be founded in Speyside. It was licensed in 1824 to Alexander Reid but, as was often the case at that period, whisky had already been produced on the farm for years. Its water originally came from Ringorm Burn, but today it is drawn from four boreholes by the River Spey, and the company owns a mile-long stretch of the River Spey to protect the supply. It also owns Easter Elchies House, as featured on every carton, built in 1700 by a Captain Grant and sensitively restored by the company in 1986.

Macallan uses low yield *Golden Promise* barley, a traditional variety which they claim maintains the high quality, flavour and consistency of their whisky. It is malted to order in a low-peat kiln at Tamdhu Maltings, and fermented with a cocktail of four yeast strains. The distillery operates a stainless steel mash tun, 16 stainless steel wash-backs, 5 wash stills and 10 spirit stills. At 1,500 litres (2,600 pints) capacity, the stills are the smallest to be directly heated by fires beneath, with rummagers to remove burnt solids and burnish the interiors, thus increasing the exposure of the low wines to copper and enhancing the flavour if the spirit. The principal feature of Macallan is that all

the whiskies are matured exclusively in Spanish oak sherry casks. These are specially selected in Jerez, having been prepared with dry oloroso sherry for one or two years. By using only the best barley and the smallest stills in Speyside, Macallan maintains the distinctive flavour of its malt whiskies – deeply rich, deliciously smooth and well-rounded, with a natural light sherry colour. The Macallan is a benchmark sherried malt whisky that simply has to be sampled.

Prior to the 1970s, Macallan's production went mainly for blending, whereas today it is sold mostly as a single malt whisky. The company wisely decided to set aside stock for marketing as a single malt, beginning in 1974 with a budget of £25. That marketing budget now exceeds £1 million a year, and "The Macallan" ranks amongst the five best-selling malt whiskies in the world. Indeed it is a tribute to their success that so many other distillers are trying to join Macallan's sherried-malt niche market, with a myriad of special wood finishes.

Our featured malt is Macallan 10 years old, which was chosen in 2001 by Michael Martin MP as the House of Commons Speaker's Malt. Other bottlings are at 7 years old selling only in Italy, 12 years old, 18 years old, Gran

Reserva, 25 years old, 30 years old, 1982 vintage and cask-strength. A range of Macallan malts, supposedly of the Twenties, Thirties, Forties and Fifties styles are both intriguing and affordable. Somewhat less affordable are the 50 years old malt, a 1942 vintage, a Millennium edition and a replica of an 1861 vintage.

The Gardener's Cottage Visitor Centre opened in 2001, offering tours, whisky tastings and a shop. Those not able to visit the distillery in person, can have a virtual browse around it at the Macallan website.

Feature	Profile
●●●●	Body
●●●	Sweetness
●	Smoky
	Medicinal
	Tobacco
●●	Honey
●	Spicy
●●●●	Winey
●●	Nutty
●●	Malty
●●●	Fruity
●	Floral

Age 10 years
Strength 40%
Nose Toffee sweet with dried fruits, cloves and sherry
Taste Smooth and well-rounded fruity flavour with honeyed sherry and oak evident, and a whiff of smoke
Cluster A Full-bodied, medium-sweet, pronounced sherry with fruity, spicy, malty notes and nutty, smoky hints
Similar to Glendronach, Royal Lochnagar, Dailuaine

MANNOCHMORE

{*man-och*-MORE}

The distillery draws its process water from the Bardon Burn, and cooling water from the Gedloch Burn. It operates a cast iron mash tun, 8 larch washbacks and 6 steam-heated stills. At one time the distillery also produced an undistinguished Loch Dhu black whisky, using a special double-charred cask preparation process, but this has since ceased being issued.

Mannochmore distillery was built in 1971 on the same site as Glenlossie distillery, and was originally intended to produce Haig blends. It is a large, modern complex which lacks character, but has a high production capacity. The emblem on the bottle is a greater spotted woodpecker, and these can sometimes be heard drilling in the Millbusies Woods nearby.

Mannochmore Single Malt whisky is available at 12 years old (profiled) in Guinness UDV's Flora and Fauna range, in the "Rare Malts" series at 22 years old (60.1%), and from some independents. It is still used in Haig and Dimple blends, which account for the bulk of its production.

Mannochmore distillery does not have a visitor centre or offer tours.

Feature	Profile
●●	Body
●	Sweetness
●	Smoky
	Medicinal
	Tobacco
●	Honey
●	Spicy
●	Winey
●●	Nutty
●	Malty
●●	Fruity
●●	Floral

Age 12 years
Strength 43%
Nose Light, aromatic and floral with a hint of smoke
Taste Fruity and creamy, with hints of honey, oak and spice
Cluster D Light, medium-sweet, low or no peat, with fruity, floral, malty notes and nutty hints
Similar to Speyside, Aultmore, Glen Grant

SPEYSIDE
SINGLE MALT SCOTCH WHISKY

MANNOCHMORE

distillery stands a few miles south of Elgin in Morayshire. The nearby Millbuies Woods are rich in birdlife, including the Great Spotted Woodpecker. The distillery draws process water from the Bardon Burn, which has its source in the MANNOCH HILLS, and cooling water from the Gedloch Burn and the Burn of Foths. Mannochmore single MALT WHISKY has a light, fruity aroma and a smooth, mellow taste.

AGED **12** YEARS

MILTONDUFF

{*mill-ton*-DUFF}

Miltonduff distillery was established in 1824 by Andrew Pearey and Donald Bain, near the Benedictine Priory of Pluscarden, beside the Black Burn. Alfred Barnard recorded that in the fifteenth century the Black Burn was blessed by the Abbot of Pluscarden, and the life-giving beverage distilled therefrom was thus christened "aqua vitae". This was an area rich in illicit distillation. At the beginning of the eighteenth century there were more than 50 unlicensed stills here, because the hills form a triangle that allowed a mutual signalling system to warn of any approaching Excise officers.

The distillery draws its water from the Black Burn which flows through the peat of Black Hill, and operates a stainless steel mash tun, 16 stainless steel washbacks and 6 stills. Hiram Walker rebuilt it in 1975, installing 2 Lomond stills which have since been removed. The whisky is matured in American bourbon oak casks and refills, stored in warehouses at the distillery.

Miltonduff Single Highland Malt whisky is available at 15 years old (profiled), and from Gordon & MacPhail. The whisky is used in various blends, notably Ballantine's.

The distillery does not have a visitor centre or offer tours.

Feature	Profile
●●	Body
●●●●	Sweetness
●	Smoky
	Medicinal
	Tobacco
●	Honey
	Spicy
	Winey
●●	Nutty
●	Malty
●	Fruity
●●	Floral

Age 15 years
Strength 46%
Nose Sweet, with a hint of honey and a whiff of smoke
Taste Very sweet with nutty, floral notes, and some fruit and honey
Cluster G Medium-bodied, sweet, low peat and floral notes
Similar to Dufftown, Speyburn, Glen Spey

MORTLACH

{MORT-*lack*}

Mortlach distillery was built on the site of an illicit still in the early nineteenth century and, in 1823, was licensed to James Findlater, the first legal distiller in Dufftown. Its water was originally drawn from Highland John's Well, a source disputed with Dufftown distillery, but today it is supplied by springs in the Conval Hills. William Grant worked here for twenty years as a clerk, before leaving to build Glenfiddich distillery nearby in 1886. The emblem on the Mortlach bottle is the shy goosander, a crested duck that nests and fishes on the River Dullan.

The distillery was expanded in 1897 when a private railway line, shared with Glendullan distillery, was installed linking it to Dufftown Station. It was fully modernized in the 1990s, and now operates a stainless steel mash tun, 6 Oregon pine washbacks and 6 steam-heated copper stills. Cooling is by 6 exterior copper worm tubs, the lyne pipes feeding into a large serpentine coil that becomes progressively narrower as it progresses down the tub.

The cooling water rising up the tub ensures that it is coldest at the end of the process. This slow, gentle way of condensing the spirit, extending its reflux with the copper, combined with slow fermentation of up to four days, contributes to the fine flavour and character of the resulting spirit. The whisky is matured in sherry casks for 16 years, which accounts for its pronounced sherry flavour and its classification alongside Macallan.

Mortlach malt whisky, or "Mortie" as it is known locally, is one of Guinness UDV's best kept secrets. Denied its rightful place in their "Classic Malts of Scotland" range, virtually all the production is used for blending, notably in their best-selling Johnnie Walker labels. However, the malt can be obtained in Guinness UDV's Flora and Fauna range at 16 years old (profiled), and also in the Rare Malts series at 20 years old cask-strength (62.2%). Other versions are available through independent bottlers.

Mortlach distillery does not have a visitor centre or offer tours.

Feature	Profile
●●●	Body
●●	Sweetness
●●	Smoky
	Medicinal
	Tobacco
●●	Honey
●●●	Spicy
●●●	Winey
●●	Nutty
●	Malty
●●	Fruity
●●	Floral

Age 16 years
Strength 43%
Nose Fruity, smoky and aromatic
Taste Full-bodied with pronounced sherry, honey and spice notes. Well-balanced fruity flavour and finish
Cluster A Full-bodied, medium-sweet, pronounced sherry with fruity, spicy, malty notes and nutty, smoky hints
Similar to Royal Lochnagar, Dailuaine, Dalmore

SPEYSIDE
SINGLE MALT
SCOTCH WHISKY

MORTLACH

was the first of seven
distilleries in Dufftown. In the
C_{19}^{th} farm animals kept in
adjoining byres were fed on
barley left over from processing
Today water from springs in
the CONVAL HILLS is used to
produce this delightful
smooth, fruity single
MALT SCOTCH WHISKY.

AGED 16 YEARS

Distilled & Bottled in SCOTLAND
MORTLACH DISTILLERY
Dufftown, Keith, Banffshire, Scotland

43% vol   70 cl

OBAN

{OH-*bun*}

Oban, Gaelic for the "little bay of caves", is a sheltered harbour town in the West Highlands. It is the gateway to the Isles and is steeped in Viking and Gaelic history. The distillery was founded in 1794 by Hugh Stevenson, a local merchant and entrepreneur, and is situated in the heart of the old town. It is the oldest and smallest of the Classic Malts distilleries. It was rebuilt in 1890–94 by J. Walter Higgin and, during excavation, a cave containing human bones and artefacts dating from the Mesolithic era (4,500–3,000 BC) was discovered in the Creag a'Bharrain Cliffs behind the distillery.

The distillery draws its water from a loch above the town and operates a small stainless steel mash tun, 4 European larch washbacks and 2 lampglass-shaped stills. The stills, which are amongst the smallest in Scotland, have unusually short lyne arms due to the cramped space of the still house. The relatively high contact with copper, due to the size of the stills and the use of a traditional copper worm condenser, creates a rich spirit that has lots of character.

Oban Single West Highland Malt is matured in American oak bourbon casks, resulting in a whisky that displays the subtle character of the spirit unmasked by excessive cask or peat flavours. The featured malt is Oban 14 years old from Guinness UDV's Classic Malts range. Oban Single Malt is also available in limited editions, such as a 1985 Distillers Edition finished in Montilla Fino Sherry casks.

The visitor centre in the old maltings has been completely redesigned, winning a five-star tourism rating. It is open all year and has an exhibition and audio-visual presentation about the history and growth of the town and its distillery. Tours of the distillery and tastings are available.

Feature	Profile
●●	Body
●●	Sweetness
●●	Smoky
●●	Medicinal
	Tobacco
	Honey
●●	Spicy
	Winey
●●	Nutty
●●	Malty
●●	Fruity
	Floral

Age 14 years
Strength 43%
Nose Salty, malty and sweet, with a discernible smokiness
Taste Rich, medium-bodied, quite sweet and peaty with citric fruits, honey and spices evident
Cluster H Medium-bodied, medium-sweet, with smoky, fruity, spicy notes and floral, nutty hints
Similar to Balblair, Craigellachie, Old Pulteney

OLD FETTERCAIRN

{old-FETTER-care'n}

Old Fettercairn distillery was founded in 1824 by Sir Alexander Ramsay on the site of a former corn mill. It is the second distillery to be licensed in Scotland, but is believed to have operated as an illicit still in the mountains long before that date. It was rebuilt in 1890 after a fire and extended to 4 stills in 1966. William Ewart Gladstone, who lived nearby at the castle of Fasque 1830–51, went on to serve 4 terms as prime minister between 1868–94, promoting legislation that greatly helped the whisky industry. Queen Victoria visited Fettercairn in 1861 during one of her Scottish tours, and this is commemorated by an arch in the town.

The distillery draws its water from springs in the Grampian mountains, and uses lightly peated malted barley supplied to order. It is a traditional distillery, operating a copper domed cast iron mashtun, 8 Oregon pine washbacks and 4 small pot stills. The whisky is matured in a mixture of bourbon American oak casks, European sherry casks and refills, stored in warehouses at the distillery.

Old Fettercairn Single Highland Malt is available at 10 years old, and in limited editions such as a 26 years old Stillman's Dram (45%). The whisky is also used in many blends.

The visitor centre and shop are open between May and September, and offer an audio-visual presentation, distillery tours and tastings.

Feature	Profile
●	Body
●●	Sweetness
●●	Smoky
	Medicinal
●	Tobacco
●●	Honey
●●	Spicy
●	Winey
●●	Nutty
●●●	Malty
●	Fruity
●	Floral

Age 10 years
Strength 43%
Nose Rather sweet and malty, with fruit and floral notes
Taste Medium to light body, nutty and spicy, with some peat and hints of autumn fruits, honey and sherry
Cluster F Medium-bodied, medium-sweet, low peat, malty notes and sherry, honey, spicy hints
Similar to Ardmore, Deanston, Tomatin

OLD PULTENEY

{*old*-PULT-*nay*}

Pulteney distillery is in Wick, at the most northerly tip of mainland Scotland, about eighteen miles from John O'Groats, in a rugged, windswept, sea-pounded area surrounded by ancient ruined castles. Wick is the Viking name for an opening or bay.

Founded in 1826, and named after Sir William Johnson Pulteney, the distillery has close links with the local fishing industry. In the nineteenth century, Wick was one of the world's busiest herring fishing ports. Over 10,000 people were employed in the industry and a thousand boats could be harboured at Wick. Many a dram of Old Pulteney was savoured when the fleet was in and the kippers were smoking. The distillery has played a prominent role in the community and the sea breeze and salty air are evident in the taste of Old Pulteney Single Malt whisky. This association is also celebrated by the emblem on the bottle – a nineteenth-century herring boat the "Isabella Fortuna", which is Scotland's oldest remaining fishing boat.

The distillery operates a cast iron mash tun, 6 stainless steel washbacks and 2 stills. The distinctively concentrated flavour of Old Pulteney whisky may be attributed to the use of a purifier above the spirit still.

It has been dubbed the "Manzanilla of the North" for its uniquely salty and beguiling aroma. Old Pulteney Single Malt whisky is available at 12 years old (profiled), at 18 years old cask strength (59.9%) and at 26 years old (46%).

The visitor centre and shop are open all year, but appointments are advisable for visits between September and April. The tour includes a presentation of the seafaring history of Wick and its distillery, and a whisky tasting. A virtual tour is also available at the distillery's website.

Feature	Profile
●●	Body
●	Sweetness
●●	Smoky
●●	Medicinal
●	Tobacco
	Honey
●	Spicy
●	Winey
●●	Nutty
●●	Malty
●●	Fruity
●●	Floral

Age 12 years
Strength 40%
Nose Delicate light aroma, with a whiff of smoke and the North Sea
Taste Creamy smooth, medium-dry with light sherry and fruit notes
Cluster H Medium-bodied, medium-sweet, with smoky, fruity, spicy notes and floral, nutty hints
Similar to Craigellachie, Oban, Glenmorangie

Left: *The original buildings and workforce at the end of the nineteenth century.*

ROYAL BRACKLA

{*royal*-BRACK-*la*}

Royal Brackla distillery was built in 1812 by William Fraser on the Cawdor estate, which is the setting for Shakespeare's *Macbeth*, Thane of Cawdor. In 1835 William IV granted Brackla a Royal warrant – the first distillery to enjoy this distinction – proclaiming it to be his favourite whisky. The warrant was renewed by Queen Victoria in 1838, for it is indeed a whisky fit for King and Thane.

The distillery was modernized in 1965, extended in 1970 and further improved in 1997. It draws its process water from the Cursack Springs above Cawdor Castle, and uses lightly-peated malted *Chalice* barley supplied to order by maltsters. It operates a large stainless steel mash tun, 6 Oregon pine washbacks, and 4 large stills. The whisky is matured in ex-bourbon American oak casks.

Royal Brackla was sold with the Dewar's portfolio to Bacardi in 1999, but, at present, its malt whisky can only be obtained under the former United Distillers' labels, for which lightly-peated barley was used to give the whisky a slightly smoky note. The emblem on the bottle is the siskin, a shy bird that feeds on conifer seeds on the Cawdor estate. It is to be hoped that the new owners will soon realise the potential of this excellent malt whisky and have it bottled under a house label.

Royal Brackla Single Malt is available at 10 years old (profiled) in Guinness UDV's Flora and Fauna range, in their Rare Malts series at 20 years old (59.8%) and from independents. A new edition is due to become available in late-2002. It is used in Dewar's White Label blend, which accounts for the bulk of its production. The future whiskies are likely to be less peaty than the present version.

The distillery does not have a visitor centre or offer tours.

Feature	Profile
●●	Body
●●●	Sweetness
●●	Smoky
●	Medicinal
●	Tobacco
●	Honey
●●	Spicy
●	Winey
	Nutty
●●	Malty
●●●	Fruity
●●	Floral

Age 10 years
Strength 43%
Nose Fresh, floral and grassy, with a whiff of smoke
Taste Sweet and creamy, with lots of fruit, malt and oaky vanilla, and spice in the finish
Cluster C Medium-bodied, medium-sweet, with fruity, floral, honey, malty notes and spicy hints
Similar to Benriach, Linkwood, Glen Ord

HIGHLAND
SINGLE MALT SCOTCH WHISKY

ROYAL BRACKLA

distillery, established in 1812, *it* lies on the *southern* shore of the MORAY FIRTH at *Cawdor* near *Nairn*. Woods around the *distillery* are home to the *SISKIN*; although a *shy bird*, it can often be seen *feeding* on *conifer seeds*.

a *Royal Warrant* was granted to the *distillery* by King William *IV* who enjoyed the *fresh, grassy, fruity* aroma of this *single malt whisky*.

AGED **10** YEARS

ROYAL LOCHNAGAR

{*royal*-LOCH-*na*-GAR}

Situated in a spectacular setting beside the River Dee, close to the Royal Palace of Balmoral, Royal Lochnagar distillery is a Highland gem. In 1848, Lochnagar's manager John Begg wrote to Queen Victoria inviting her to visit the distillery and sample his whisky. The Queen and Prince Albert arrived without warning, toured the distillery and sampled their first dram. The royal warrant was quickly granted, one of the fastest on record, and Royal Lochnagar has been enjoyed by generations of the Royal Family and their Balmoral staff for over 150 years. Indeed, it was Queen Victoria's enthusiasm for whisky, following her visit to the Lochnagar distillery, that helped create the international demand for "Scotch" whisky.

Royal Lochnagar's mash tun and 2 elegant copper stills, shaped like upturned wine glasses, are much the same as in Victorian times, though the distillery and visitor centre have been recently modernized. Process water is drawn from a spring on Lochnagar Mountain. The distillery uses lightly-peated barley and operates 2 larch washbacks with an unusually long 70 hours fermentation time. The output from both stills is condensed using traditional copper worm tubs in cooling barrels outside the stillhouse. The whisky is matured in American bourbon casks and a few European oak sherry butts, stored in warehouses at the site. In addition to the profiled 12 years old, Royal Lochnagar Single Highland Malt whisky is also available as a limited edition "Selected Reserve" (43%) and in Guinness UDV's Rare Malts series at 23 years old (59.7%).

Visitors can enjoy a guided tour, sample the Royal dram and purchase a range of malts in the shop.

Feature	Profile
●●●	Body
●●	Sweetness
●●	Smoky
	Medicinal
	Tobacco
●●	Honey
●●	Spicy
●●	Winey
●●	Nutty
●●	Malty
●●●	Fruity
●	Floral

Age 12 years
Strength 40%
Nose Aromatic, smoky, with rich spicy fruit
Taste Complex, layered flavours of malt and fruit, with honey, sherry and spice also discernable
Cluster A Full-bodied, medium-sweet, pronounced sherry with fruity, spicy, malty notes and nutty, smoky hints
Similar to Dailuaine, Dalmore, Mortlach

SCAPA

{SCAPP-*ah*}

Scapa distillery was built in 1885 by John Townsend beside the Lingro Burn on the shore of Scapa Flow. It is a natural harbour that links the North Sea to the Atlantic Ocean and was used as a naval base in both World Wars. Orkney is an island steeped in history with almost 3,000 relics such as Neolithic standing stones, chambered tombs, Iron Age earth houses, a Viking palace and early Celtic monasteries. A fortified tower dating from 3000 BC stands close to the distillery and the graves of Norse warriors, buried with their swords and horses, have been found nearby. The German fleet was scuttled in Scapa Flow in 1918, and in World War II the distillery was saved from fire by the Royal Navy.

Two of the original Victorian warehouses survived, but most of the present buildings date from 1959 when it was substantially rebuilt. In the midst of its ancient history, the modern Scapa

distillery looms incongruously above the shore in an area of great natural beauty. It was once powered by a water wheel and this has been retained as a feature.

The distillery draws its hard, peaty water from the Lingro Burn and, to compensate, it uses totally unpeated malted barley. It operates a squat Lomond wash still with a short cylindrical neck that reduces reflux to produce a richer, heavy spirit, and a conventional spirit still. The whisky is matured in ex-bourbon American oak casks in warehouses beside the sea, which accounts for its distinctive vanilla and salty notes.

Scapa Single Orkney Malt whisky is available at 12 years old (profiled). Other versions can be obtained from Gordon & MacPhail, and it is used in blends such as Ballantine's.

The distillery ceased working in 1994, but visitors are welcome by prior appointment.

Feature	Profile
●●	Body
●●	Sweetness
●	Smoky
●	Medicinal
	Tobacco
●●	Honey
●	Spicy
●	Winey
●●	Nutty
●●	Malty
●●	Fruity
●●	Floral

Age 12 years
Strength 40%
Nose Floral and fruity with malt, vanilla notes and a whiff of sea air
Taste Heather honey, citrus fruits, nutty vanilla, toffee and spice
Cluster B Medium-bodied, medium-sweet, with nutty, malty, floral, honey and fruity notes
Similar to Benromach, Aberfeldy, Knockando

SPEYBURN

{*spey*-BURN}

There are many beautifully situated distilleries in Scotland, but few can surpass Speyburn, sitting majestically in a corner of the Spey Valley at the foot of the densely wooded hills, on the outskirts of the quiet Highland town of Rothes. Designed by the famous distillery architect, Charles Doig of Elgin, it is reputed to be the most photographed distillery in Scotland. It is built beside Cnock na Croiche (the "hillock of the gibbet"), the site of the Rothes gallows where criminals were hanged once.

The most distinctive feature of Speyburn is its 2- and 3- storey buildings, which use the sloping 3-acre site to best effect. With its impressive elevations and traditional pagoda chimney stretching skywards, Speyburn still commands an imposing aspect in the Glen of Rothes.

The distillery draws its soft peaty water from the Granty Burn and uses unpeated malted barley. It operates a stainless steel copper-domed mash tun, 6 Douglas fir washbacks, and 2 stills. The wash room is exceptionally cold, which allows for a slower and better fermentation. The whisky is matured in ex-bourbon American oak casks at the distillery and it was the first to install steam-powered drum maltings. The emblem on the label is a leaping salmon, a native of the Spey that has been fished so intensively that the remaining stocks need to be conserved. For every salmon caught that is returned to the river, the distillery generously rewards the angler with a free bottle of malt whisky.

Speyburn Single Highland Malt whisky is available at 10 years old (profiled), at 21 years old as a single-cask limited edition and at 27 years old in the Highland selection series. It does not have a visitor centre.

Feature	Profile
●●	Body
●●●●	Sweetness
●	Smoky
	Medicinal
	Tobacco
●●	Honey
●	Spicy
	Winey
	Nutty
●●	Malty
●	Fruity
●●	Floral

Age 10 years
Strength 40%
Nose Fresh, aromatic and malty, with a touch of smoke
Taste Medium-bodied and sweet, with a toffee, oaky note and a fruity finish
Cluster G Medium-bodied, sweet, low peat and floral notes
Similar to Miltonduff, Glenfiddich, Dufftown

SPEYSIDE

{*spey*-SIDE}

Speyside distillery is located near picturesque Kingussie, on the banks of the River Tromie which feeds into the River Spey. It is one of Scotland's newest distilleries, the dream of its founder, George Christie, and it was hand-built by Alex Fairlie, a dry stone dyker.

Construction started in 1962 and finished in 1989, but it was not until 1991 that the first spirit began to flow. The distillery draws its water from the River Tromie and only uses *Chariot* barley, lightly peated and malted to order. It operates a stainless steel mash tun, 4 stainless steel washbacks and 2 small pot stills. The smallness of the stills maximizes catalysis with the copper, resulting in a rich, fruity spirit. The whisky is matured in ex-bourbon American oak hogsheads, with a few European oak sherry butts to provide a sherried edge for the malts.

An anachronism arising from naming a distillery "Speyside", even one that lies directly beside the river Spey, is that "Speyside Single Speyside Malt" does not trip neatly off the tongue. Therefore, it is called Speyside Single Highland Malt whisky, which really goes to prove the point that classifying whiskies by region is somewhat nonsensical.

Speyside Single Highland Malt whisky is available at 10 years old (profiled), and as Drumguish, which carries no age statement. The company also produces six blended whiskies under their Speyside label, ranging from 15 to 30 years old, a Speyside Millennium 2000 edition, and two Glentromie blends.

Speyside distillery does not have a visitor centre or offer tours. Kingussie is well worth visiting, however, as is the nearby ruin of Ruthven Barracks built by the English army to control the Highlanders after the 1715 rebellion.

Feature	Profile
●●	Body
●●	Sweetness
●	Smoky
	Medicinal
	Tobacco
●	Honey
	Spicy
●	Winey
●●	Nutty
●●	Malty
●●	Fruity
●●	Floral

Age 10 years
Strength 40%
Nose Fragrant, sweet and malty with a whiff of smoke
Taste Medium-bodied, creamy with fruity and floral notes, some nuts and vanilla
Cluster D Light, medium-sweet, low or no peat, with fruity, floral, malty notes and nutty hints
Similar to Aultmore, Tamdhu, Mannochmore

SPRINGBANK

{*spring*-BANK}

Springbank distillery was first licensed in 1828, but is said to have been previously operated as an illicit still by Archibald Mitchell. It is still owned by the same family and is, therefore, the oldest independent distillery in Scotland. Springbank uniquely carries out all of the production process, from traditional floor maltings to bottling, at the one site. It is the only remaining distillery to malt all of its barley on a traditional malting floor; other distillers that have retained floor maltings are obliged to supplement their own malted barley with supplies from commercial maltsters.

Water is drawn from Crosshill Loch, which is fed by springs on Beinn Ghuilean. The distillery operates a century-old cast iron mash tun, 5 boatskin larch washbacks, and 3 medium-sized pot stills. The wash still is directly heated with rummagers to remove burnt solids and burnish the interiors. This increases the charring effect of direct flame heating and the exposure of the low wines to copper and thus enhances the flavour of the spirit. Another unusual feature is that Springbank malt whisky is partly triple-distilled, the low wines, foreshots and feints being re-distilled with a proportion of the next batch of low wines in an intermediate distillation before final distillation occurs in the spirit still. This produces a light spirit, but this is not as evident in the Springbank malts as it is in other triple-distilled whiskies. The reason for this may be that they are bottled at 46% without being chill-filtered and, thereby, retain the full character of the spirit. The whisky is matured in a mixture of ex-bourbon American oak and ex-sherry European oak casks, though bourbon casks are more heavily utilized.

Springbank Campbeltown Single Malt whisky is available at 10 years old (profiled), at 15 years old, at 21 years old, and in special editions such as a 12 years old rum cask edition (54%)

bottled in 2002. The distillery also produces a double-distilled peated Longrow single malt at 10 years old, and a separate 10 years old Longrow matured in sherry wood. There are two Springbank blends, Mitchell's 12 years old and Campbeltown Loch, and a triple-distilled unpeated Hazelburn is in prospect.

It does not have a visitor centre, but tours can be arranged in the summer by appointment. There is a shop, Eaglesome, in Campbeltown and a newsletter can be obtained directly from the distillery.

Feature	Profile
●●	Body
●●	Sweetness
●●	Smoky
●●	Medicinal
	Tobacco
●●	Honey
●●	Spicy
●	Winey
●●	Nutty
●	Malty
	Fruity
●	Floral

Age 10 years
Strength 46%
Nose Aromatic with a peaty note and hints of honey and spice
Taste Sweet and malty at first, with a salty, smoky note and a spicy finish
Cluster I Medium-light, dry, with smoky, spicy, honey notes and nutty, floral hints
Similar to Bowmore, Highland Park, Bruichladdich

STRATHISLA

{*strath*-EYE-*la*}

Set in the medieval market town of Keith, on the banks of the River Isla, Strathisla distillery claims to be the oldest distillery in the Highlands. It was founded in 1786 by George Taylor and Alexander Milne as Milton distillery, named after nearby Milton Castle. With its distinctive pagodas, cobbled courtyard, water wheel and classic, gabled granite buildings, Strathisla is one of the prettiest of the traditional distilleries and well worth visiting.

Much of its production goes for blending, and Strathisla has been dubbed the "home and heart of Chivas Regal". Its water is drawn from Broomhill Spring, a source recorded by Dominican monks in the twelfth century. It operates a stainless steel mash tun, 10 Oregon pine washbacks and 4 compact, copper pot stills, crammed into an atmospheric oak-beamed still house, and 2 delightfully original spirit safes. The whisky is matured in a mixture of American oak ex-bourbon and European sherry casks.

Strathisla single malt whisky is only available at 12 years old, as profiled. However, it is used in several blends – 12 and 18 years old Chivas Regal, Royal Salute 21 years old, Revolve 1801, Century and Oldest. Those aged 18 and 21 years contain Strathisla malt of comparable age.

The visitor centre and shop are open all year. After a self-guided tour of the distillery, visitors can relax in the congenial Isla and Dram reception rooms, and enjoy coffee and shortbread, and taste Strathisla 12 years old single malt whisky or Chivas Regal. Visitors can also nose several of the older single malt and grain whiskies that combine to create the famous Chivas Regal blends.

Feature	Profile
●●	Body
●●	Sweetness
●	Smoky
	Medicinal
	Tobacco
●●	Honey
●●	Spicy
●●	Winey
●●●	Nutty
●●●	Malty
●●●	Fruity
●●	Floral

Age 12 years
Strength 43%
Nose Meadows, spice, and a hint of peat
Taste Malty and nutty, with honeyed fruit and a spicy finish
Cluster B Medium-bodied, medium-sweet, with nutty, malty, floral, honey and fruity notes
Similar to Benromach, Aberfeldy, Blair Athol

STRATHMILL

{*strath*-MILL}

Strathmill distillery was converted from a former flour mill in 1892, at a time of great optimism in the industry, when foreign markets were opening to whisky. Although modernized and extended in the 1960s, it retains some of the original Victorian buildings in a delightful setting beside the River Isla, on the edge of Keith.

It draws its water from a spring above the distillery that flows into the Isla. The distillery operates a stainless steel mash tun, 6 stainless steel washbacks and 4 squat stills. The whisky is matured in American oak bourbon and refill casks stored in traditional warehouses at the distillery. The emblem on the bottle is a pied wagtail, which can be seen hunting on the banks of the Isla and occasionally in the distillery yard.

Strathmill Single Highland Malt whisky is available at 12 years old in Guinness UDV's Flora and Fauna series, and occasionally from independents. Most of the production goes for blending, principally in Guinness UDV's J&B blend and formerly in Alfred Dunhill's Old Master and Gentleman's Speyside blends.

Strathmill distillery does not have a visitor centre or offer tours.

Feature	Profile
●●	Body
●●●	Sweetness
●	Smoky
	Medicinal
	Tobacco
	Honey
●●	Spicy
	Winey
●●	Nutty
●	Malty
●●●	Fruity
●●	Floral

Age 12 years
Strength 43%
Nose Sweet and fragrant, with a malty note
Taste Medium bodied, sweet with apples and citrus fruits, quite nutty and spicy
Cluster H Medium-bodied, medium-sweet, with smoky, fruity, spicy notes and floral, nutty hints
Similar to Balblair, Glenmorangie, Craigellachie

SPEYSIDE
SINGLE MALT SCOTCH WHISKY

STRATHMILL

distillery was established in 1891 in a converted grain mill. The PIED WAGTAIL is a familiar sight in the distillery yard on the banks of the nearby RIVER ISLA, which provides water for cooling. A spring on the site provides processing water. This deep amber, single MALT has a light, rounded body, a sweet, sweet flavour, with a dry finish and chocolaty aftertaste.

AGED **12** YEARS

TALISKER

{TAL-*is-ker*}

Talisker is the only distillery on the island of Skye – the Misty Isle. It was built in 1830 by Hugh and Kenneth MacAskill, in the Gaelic heartland of Carbost, against the fierce protestations of the kirk Minister, the Rev. Roderick Macleod. He declared this to be "one of the greatest curses that… could befall [this] or any other place".

The distillery stands on the rocky, storm-lashed shore of Loch Harport, in the shadow of the rugged Cuillin Mountains. It was destroyed by fire in 1960, when a valve on the spirit still was accidentally left open and burning spirit ran down the Carbost Burn into Loch Harport, setting the loch itself on fire. It was rebuilt in 1962 and further renovated in 1998. It now boasts a large stainless steel mash tun with a sparkling copper top, 6 Oregon pine washbacks, 3 low wines stills, 2 wash stills with unique U-shaped lyne pipes, a fine spirit safe, and 5 wooden worm tubs.

Prior to 1998 the water supply from the Carbost Burn was frequently insufficient in periods of drought. The dam was, therefore, extended and, with the help of a water diviner, some new springs were connected. The mineral-rich water, from these springs on Cnoc na Speirag (the "Hawk Hill"), that supplies the distillery, runs through heather and peat which no doubt contribute to the whisky's robust character. The whisky is matured in American bourbon oak casks in traditional warehouses by the loch shore, whose damp old walls harbour mould growths in their dark corners.

Talisker has been available as a single malt whisky since the late nineteenth century – it was praised by Robert Louis Stevenson in 1880 as "the King o' Drinks", and was bought regularly by the Indian Army. Our featured malt, Talisker 10 years old in Guinness UDV's Classic Malts range, has won several awards in the International Wine and Spirits Competition since 1995 and three International Spirits Challenge Trophies. Talisker can also be obtained in limited editions, such as a 1986 Distillers' Edition finished in Amoroso sherry casks, a cask-strenth edition (60%) not chill-filtered, and a 25 years old single cask (59.9%) sold in numbered bottles.

The new visitor centre has an excellent exhibition on the history of the distillery and its location, and is open all year. Unusually, visitors are given a dram to taste *before* embarking on the distillery tour. From a pagoda-capped gazebo in the gardens the indigenous peregrine falcons and sparrow hawks can be seen. The very lucky may even catch a glimpse of a white-tailed sea eagle soaring over Hawk Hill, and seals basking on the rocks. Visitors can round off their visit with a dram of Talisker and a plate of Loch Harport oysters, said to be the island's harvest and the island's spirit together, in divine harmony.

Feature	Profile
●●●●	Body
●●	Sweetness
●●●	Smoky
●●●	Medicinal
	Tobacco
●	Honey
●●●	Spicy
	Winey
●	Nutty
●●	Malty
●●	Fruity
	Floral

Age 10 years
Strength 45.8%
Nose Slightly sweet, peaty and salty – powerful island aroma
Taste Rich, full-bodied, pungent with sea-shore, barley-malt flavours, peppered spice and dried-fruit notes
Cluster J Full-bodied, dry, pungent, peaty and medicinal, with spicy, tobacco notes
Similar to Caol Ila, Clynelish, Ardbeg

TAMDHU

{TAM-*doo*}

Tamdhu distillery was built at Knockando village in the boom of 1897 by William Grant, a director of Highland Distillers. The site was chosen for its plentiful supply of clear spring water and proximity to the Great North of Scotland railway line. After the railway closed in the 1960s, Knockando station was converted into a visitor centre for Alfred Dunhill who used it to promote their blends. The distillery was extended in the 1970s to 6 stills, but it is the Tamdhu maltings that are of most interest. This is the only Speyside distillery that malts its own barley, producing enough to meet its own needs and those of its parent group and several other Speyside distilleries.

The maltings use long concrete trenches, called Saladin boxes, in which the germinating barley is turned mechanically every nine to twelve hours for five days. The floor of the box is perforated and humid air is circulated through the barley to maintain its temperature at 66°C. The whole process is computer controlled, requiring only one operator to supervise several batches simultaneously. Once the barley has germinated, it is dried in hot air

with any specified amount of peat smoke introduced to order, according to the distiller's peating requirements.

The distillery draws its water from a well below the building and the Tamdhu Burn is used for cooling water. It operates a stainless steel mash tun, 9 Oregon pine washbacks and 6 conventional pot stills. The whisky is matured in a

mixture of American bourbon, European sherry and refill casks.

Tamdhu Single Malt whisky is available at 10 years old (profiled), and at other ages from Gordon & MacPhail, Cadenhead and Signatory. The whisky is used in the Famous Grouse blend, in Famous Grouse Vintage Malt, and in the Alfred Dunhill blends currently popular in America.

Tamdhu visitor centre is not at present open for tours.

Feature	Profile
●	Body
●●	Sweetness
●	Smoky
	Medicinal
	Tobacco
●●	Honey
	Spicy
●	Winey
●	Nutty
●●	Malty
●●	Fruity
●●	Floral

Age 10 years
Strength 40%
Nose Fruity, floral and honeyed with a little smoke
Taste Light, slightly sweet, with malty, toffee notes and a hint of S```herry
Cluster D Light, medium-sweet, low or no peat, with fruity, floral, malty notes and nutty hints
Similar to Speyside, Tobermory, Aultmore

TAMNAVULIN

{TAM-*na*-VOO-*lin*}

Tamnavulin is Gaelic for "mill on the hill" as it was built on the site of a former woollen mill in the Glen of Livet. The distillery was completed in 1966 beside the Allt a Choire (Corrie stream) a tributary of the river Livet. It is a very modern distillery with a rather bleak, functional look. The exception is the old mill visitor centre with its water wheel, described as the "nicest centre on the whisky trail" by the Northern Scot magazine.

It draws its water from underground springs at Easterton and its cooling water from the Allt a Choire. It operates a stainless steel mash tun, 4 large stainless steel washbacks with a capacity of 69,000 litres (121,000 pints) and 6 stills. It is fully computerized and can be run by a small team. The whisky is matured in bourbon American oak and refill casks in modern warehouses at the distillery, where the casks are racked twelve high.

Tamnavulin Single Speyside Malt whisky is available at 12 years old (profiled) and at 24 and 28 years old as the Stillman's Dram. The label states that it is "naturally light". Other versions are available from independents, such as a cask-strength bottling by Cadenhead matured in sherry wood. The whisky is also used in Whyte & Mackay, Mackinlay and Crawfords blends.

Tamnavulin distillery has converted the former mill into an attractive visitor centre, which is also featured on the label of the malt whisky. Visitors are shown a short video film about the making of whisky and given a guided tour of the distillery and tastings. It also has a shop and a landscaped picnic area set in spectacular scenery. At the time of writing both the distillery and visitor centre were closed, but it is hoped that they will re-open in the near future.

Feature	Profile
●	Body
●●●	Sweetness
●●	Smoky
	Medicinal
	Tobacco
	Honey
●●	Spicy
	Winey
●●	Nutty
●	Malty
●●	Fruity
●●●	Floral

Age 12 years
Strength 40%
Nose Fragrant, floral and fruity with a whiff of smoke
Taste Light and sweet, with nutty, floral notes, some citrus fruit, grass, spice and a light smokiness
Cluster H Medium-bodied, medium-sweet, with smoky, fruity, spicy notes and floral, nutty hints
Similar to Craigellachie Balblair, Glenmorangie

TEANINICH

{TEA-*an-in-ich*}

Teaninich distillery was founded by Captain Hugh Munro in 1817 on his own land, but has lately been overrun by a modern industrial estate as Alness expanded. One of the earliest to be licensed, it initially struggled against illicit competition, but by 1830 had become a thriving business. It was extended and refitted in 1899, power being supplied by two water wheels fed from a dam, later supplemented by a steam engine. These continued to be the main source of power until the 1960s, when it was converted to electricity with steam-heated stills. In 1970 a new still house with 6 stills was added, and the milling, mashing and fermentation unit was rebuilt in 1973.

The emblem on the bottle is a porpoise, examples of which can be seen in the Cromarty Firth nearby. Teaninich's process and cooling water is drawn from Dairywell Spring.

The whisky is matured in American bourbon and European sherry casks in warehouses on the site. Most is used for blends such as Dimple, Haig and Vat 69. Teaninich Single Malt (profiled) is available at 10 years old in Guinness UDV's Flora and Fauna range, in the Rare Malts series at 23 years old (57.3%), and 27 years old (64.2%), and from some independents. It does not have a visitor centre or offer tours.

Feature	Profile
●●	Body
●●	Sweetness
●●	Smoky
●	Medicinal
	Tobacco
	Honey
●●	Spicy
	Winey
	Nutty
	Malty
●●	Fruity
●●	Floral

Age 10 years
Strength 43%
Nose Fresh, fruity and grassy, with a hint of peat
Taste Citrus, floral and spice notes, and some smoke
Cluster H Medium-bodied, medium-sweet, with smoky, fruity, spicy notes and floral, nutty hints
Similar to Glenmorangie, Balblair, Glen Garioch

HIGHLAND
SINGLE MALT
SCOTCH WHISKY

The *Cromarty Firth* is one of the few places in the British Isles inhabited by *PORPOISE*. They can be seen quite regularly, swimming close to the shore less than a mile from

TEANINICH

distillery. Founded in 1817 in the *Ross-shire* town of ALNESS, the *distillery* is now one of the largest in *Scotland.* TEANINICH is an assertive *single MALT WHISKY* with a *spicy,* smoky, *satisfying* taste.

AGED **10** YEARS

43% vol

Distilled & Bottled in SCOTLAND
TEANINICH DISTILLERY,
Alness, Ross-shire, Scotland

70cl

TOBERMORY

{TOBER-*more-ay*}

Tobermory distillery, was originally established as Ledaig distillery in 1798 by John Sinclair, a local merchant, and was first licensed in 1823. It is set in the attractive fishing village of Tobermory, at the northern tip of the island of Mull.

It has had a chequered history, going in and out of ownership, sometimes operating but frequently silent. It used to produce a heavily-peated malt, and this has continued under the Ledaig label. More recently, the Tobermory label has been reserved for an unpeated expression, though a whiff of smoke is evident from the water.

It draws its water from a private loch on the hill above the distillery and uses unpeated malted barley for its principal Tobermory malt whisky. The distillery was substantially upgraded in the 1990s and is now capable of producing a million litres of spirit a year.

It operates a traditional copper-domed cast-iron mash tun, 4 Oregon pine washbacks and 4 medium sized stills with unique lyne arms. The whisky is matured in a mixture of bourbon American oak and European sherry oak casks, in warehouses on the mainland.

Tobermory Single Malt whisky is available at 10 years old (profiled) and as a heavily-peated version called Ledaig at 15 and 20 years old. Earlier versions of Ledaig are still available from independents such as Cadenhead.

The visitor centre and shop are open all year, though appointments are advisable between October and April. It offers a video about the history of Tobermory, guided tours and tastings.

Feature	Profile
●	Body
●	Sweetness
●	Smoky
	Medicinal
	Tobacco
●	Honey
	Spicy
	Winey
●	Nutty
● ●	Malty
● ●	Fruity
● ●	Floral

Age 10 years
Strength 40%
Nose Delicately aromatic and malty, with a whiff of smoke
Taste Light, medium dry with fruity and floral notes, and a hint of honey and spice
Cluster D Light, medium-sweet, low or no peat, with fruity, floral, malty notes and nutty hints
Similar to Aultmore, Tamdhu, Speyside

TOMATIN

*{tom-*AH-*tin}*

Tomatin is Gaelic for "hill of the juniper bushes", which describes its pretty setting in the Monadhliath mountains. At 1,030 feet (315 metres) above sea level, it is one of the highest distilleries in Scotland. It was built during the Victorian boom of 1897 and expanded from its original 2 stills to 23 stills by 1974. It was then Scotland's largest malt whisky distillery, capable of producing 13 million litres (7½ million pints) of alcohol a year, but this is no longer the case since some of the stills have been removed. The buildings are mostly of industrial design, although some from the original distillery have been retained, including a nineteenth-century dunnage warehouse with blackened stone walls and an earth floor.

The distillery's water flows over the quartz and granite of the Monadhliath mountains, through peat bogs and heather into the Allt-na-Frithe (the "free burn"). It operates a semi-Lauter stainless steel mash tun, 12 stainless steel washbacks and 12 small pot stills; the others have been de-commissioned. The stills have boil balls incorporated in the necks, with a pinched waist, to encourage reflux. Tomatin also has its own cooperage, where casks are built and maintained by coopers. At 65,000 litres (14,300 gallons) of spirit per week, it is one of the largest proucers of malt whisky in Scotland. Tomatin whisky is mostly matured in ex-bourbon American oak casks, with a few sherry butts to give a sherried note to the malts.

Tomatin Single Highland Malt whisky is available at 10 years old (profiled), and at 25 years old. The company also produces several blends, including Talisman, 5 years old "Big T", and two Antiquary de luxe blends aged 12 and 21 years old.

The visitor centre and shop are open all year round. The centre offers a short video film, tours and tastings.

Feature	Profile
●●	Body
●●●	Sweetness
●●	Smoky
	Medicinal
	Tobacco
●●	Honey
●●	Spicy
●	Winey
●	Nutty
●●	Malty
	Fruity
●	Floral

Age 10 years
Strength 40%
Nose Aromatic and sweet, with malt and light smoke notes
Taste Vanilla, honey and spice. A long nutty, liquorice finish and a hint of sherry
Cluster F Medium-bodied, medium-sweet, low peat, malty notes and Ssherry, honey, spicy hints
Similar to Ardmore, Old Fettercairn, Glen Deveron

TOMINTOUL

*{tom-in-*TOWEL}

Tomintoul is a modern distillery built in 1965 and extended in 1974. Its functional, industrial buildings are situated in the beautifully wooded valley of Avonside near Tomintoul, the highest village in Scotland.

It draws its water from Ballantruan Spring and its malted barley is delivered lightly-peated to order. It operates a large semi-Lauter mash tun, 6 stainless steel washbacks and 4 tall stills incorporating boil balls in the neck to increase reflux. The size of the stills and the use of boil balls account for the lightness of the resulting spirit. The whisky is matured in a mixture of ex-bourbon American oak casks, refill hogsheads and a few oloroso sherry oak butts, hence its lightly sherried note.

Tomintoul Single Speyside Malt whisky is available at 10 years old (profiled), with other versions in prospect under the new management, though the bulk of the production goes for blending. A 26 years old edition can be obtained from Gordon & MacPhail and Signatory.

Although the distillery does not have a visitor centre or shop, visitors are welcome by appointment.

Feature	Profile
	Body
●●●	Sweetness
●	Smoky
	Medicinal
	Tobacco
●●	Honey
●●	Spicy
●	Winey
●	Nutty
●●	Malty
●	Fruity
●●	Floral

Age 10 years
Strength 40%
Nose Light, fragrant and grassy, with a malty edge
Taste Quite sweet with oaky vanilla and spice notes, and hints of citrus fruits and sherry
Cluster E Light, medium-sweet, low peat, with floral, malty notes and fruity, spicy, honey hints
Similar to Inchgower, Glenlossie, Glenallachie

TOMINTOUL
Speyside
SINGLE MALT
Scotch Whisky
AGED **10** YEARS

DISTILLED AND BOTTLED IN SCOTLAND
TOMINTOUL DISTILLERY,
BALLINDALLOCH, BANFFSHIRE, SCOTLAND.

PRODUCT OF SCOTLAND
SINGLE
70cl *Highland* 40%vol
MALT

TORMORE

{tor-MORE}

Tormore distillery was designed in 1958 by the architect Sir Albert Richardson, a past president of the Royal Academy better known for restoring Georgian mansions. It is set on a slope with panoramic views over Speyside and the Cromdale Hills. The main production buildings are arranged around a square courtyard, fronted by an ornamental lake with fountains, flanked by gardens and topiary stills. In winter the fountain was removed and the lake used as a curling rink. In the belfry to the right is an unusual clock that chimes "Highland Laddie" on the hour, followed by "Coming through the Rye", "Corn Rigs" and "Bonnie Lass of Fyvie" at the quarter-hours. The distillery manager's house to the left and workers' houses at the rear are white-harled with margined windows and doors. Built for Long John Distillers as a showcase distillery during the 1950s, its production capacity was doubled in 1972 to 8 stills.

It draws its soft water from Achvochkie Burn, which flows down granite hills and through peat and heather, rising cold and crystal clear above the distillery. It operates a large stainless steel Lauter mash tun, 8 stainless steel washbacks and 8 relatively large stills. The whisky is matured in refill casks, mostly American oak, stored in 6 warehouses behind the distillery.

Tormore Single Speyside Malt whisky is difficult to find but has been available at 10 years old (profiled), and at 15 years old (46%) through Gordon and MacPhail and other independents. Most of its production is used in blends such as Ballantine's, Teachers, Long John and Stewart's Cream of the Barley.

It is a pity the distillery does not have a visitor centre, for its twentieth-century architectural design is unique and was intended as a showcase. Visitors are welcome by appointment, however, and open days are occasionally organized through the Moray Society.

Feature	Profile
●●	Body
●●	Sweetness
●	Smoky
	Medicinal
	Tobacco
●	Honey
	Spicy
●	Winey
●●	Nutty
●	Malty
	Fruity
	Floral

Age 10 years
Strength 43%
Nose Light and nutty, with hints of honey and sherry
Taste Slightly sweet, malty with a whiff of smoke
Cluster F Medium-bodied, medium-sweet, low peat, malty notes and sherry, honey, spicy hints
Similar to Ardmore, Glenrothes, Glen Keith

TULLIBARDINE

{*tully*-BAR-*deen*}

Tullibardine distillery was built in 1949 at Blackford in southern Perthshire, to a functional design by the architect William Delmé Evans. The district is historically famous – and *infamous* – for its water. Legend has it that the twelfth-century Norwegian King Magnus lost his wife Helen, while attempting to cross the River Allan nearby. The drowned queen was buried at the scene and her grave is still visible at Deaf Knowe near the ford, hence the village was named Blackford.

The distillery is named after Tullibardine Moor, famous as the home of the Gleneagles Hotel and its championship golf courses. It was built on the site of an ancient brewery that is supposed to have supplied beer for the coronation of James IV at Scone in 1488. Another Tullibardine distillery operated from a farm near Blackford at the turn of the nineteenth century, but its precise location is not known. Two brands of Scottish mineral water are bottled from the same source – Highland Spring and Gleneagles.

Tullibardine distillery draws its soft, clear water from Danny Burn, the same spring that supplied the medieval brewery. It operates a stainless steel mash tun, 4 Oregon pine washbacks

and four stills. The whiskies are matured in American oak hogsheads, some of which have been seasoned with sherry, and are stored in warehouses at the site.

Tullibardine Single Highland Malt whisky is available at 10 years old (profiled) and at 30 years old as the Stillman's Dram. Other versions are available through independents.

The distillery does not have a visitor centre or offer tours.

Feature	Profile
●●	Body
●●●	Sweetness
	Smoky
	Medicinal
●	Tobacco
	Honey
●●	Spicy
●	Winey
●	Nutty
●●	Malty
●●	Fruity
●	Floral

Age 10 years
Strength 40%
Nose Fragrant, sweet
and malty
Taste Creamy texture with
some spice, hints of sherry
and nuts, and a fruity finish
Cluster F Medium-bodied,
medium-sweet, low peat,
malty notes and sherry, honey,
spicy hints
Similar to Glen Keith,
Glenrothes, Auchroisk

IDENTIFYING MALT WHISKIES

The standard flavour profile may now be used to identify the character of other whiskies not reviewed in this book. For example, the whiskies of Ireland, Japan, New Zealand, Canada, USA, Sweden and Wales could be profiled, as could other products of the Scottish distilleries, independent bottlings and own-label supermarket malts.

The flavour profile of any whisky can be specified in the form below to identify its cluster type. The score for each feature is entered into TypeAnalyst, a computer program that finds the cluster that fits it best and any whiskies that are similar in flavour.

Understanding whisky character is fundamental to developing brands with enhanced consumer appeal. A malt whisky is conspicuous in its use and thereby contributes to the user's lifestyle. John McGrath, Chief Executive of Diageo, puts it simply:

"You have to know a brand to grow a brand". Brand management includes defining a product's personality, or how it is viewed by consumers, and differentiating it from the competition.

The flavour character of a malt whisky is one aspect of the brand's personality, though arguably the most important because it is ultimately a drink to be savoured in company. The bottle, labels and packaging add to its appeal because it must look good in a bar, drinks cabinet or on a table. Advertising slogans and any special product focus also help to express the brand's personality. The distillery is important too because, unlike most other spirits, a single malt whisky is uniquely identified with where it is made and the people who make it. Price is important because heavy discounting can stimulate sales but also devalue a brand's quality image.

Sensory Feature	None	Hint	Medium	Definite	Full
Body/Weight	0	1	2	3	4
Sweetness	0	1	2	3	4
Peaty/Smoky	0	1	2	3	4
Medicinal/Salty	0	1	2	3	4
Tobacco/Feinty	0	1	2	3	4
Honey/Vanilla	0	1	2	3	4
Spicy/Woody	0	1	2	3	4
Sherry/Winey	0	1	2	3	4
Nutty/Creamy	0	1	2	3	4
Malty/Cereal	0	1	2	3	4
Fruity/Estery	0	1	2	3	4
Floral/Herbal	0	1	2	3	4

The flavour character of the whiskies presented in this book can, therefore, contribute to brand management, competitor analysis, marketing and differentiation. Retailers can use it to advise customers when contemplating a malt whisky purchase. But its main purpose is to guide consumers through the complexities and delights of the great malt whiskies of Scotland.

THE SCOTCH WHISKY HERITAGE CENTRE

The Scotch Whisky Heritage Centre was established in 1988 in a former Victorian school, at an ideal location on The Royal Mile next to Edinburgh Castle. Together with the Castle, the Royal Yacht Brittania and the Museum for Scotland, it is one of four tourist attractions in Edinburgh awarded five stars by the Scottish Tourist Board. It is co-owned by the whisky producers of Scotland, with a mission to promote Scotch whisky worldwide, and attracts around 250 thousand visitors a year.

The Centre runs guided tours seven days a week, with multi-lingual guides in eight languages and Braille, starting with a whisky tasting. The history and process of making whisky is described in three short films. An exhibition includes a scale model of Tormore distillery, a walk-through washback, pot and coffey stills, and a barrel ride that illustrates 300 years of whisky history. There is an opportunity to nose new spirit as well as malt and grain whiskies, and you'll meet the ghost of a former master blender who reveals the secrets of the art of blending whisky and the "angel's share".

After your tour you can relax in the Whisky Bond Bar, which stocks over 270 different Scotch whisky brands, and join the Scotch Whisky Appreciation Society which now has over 6,000 members worldwide. The adjoining restaurant offers good home cooking, including hot meals, light snacks, tea and coffee. Nearly all the malt whiskies profiled in *Whisky Classified* can be purchased in the shop, which also sells special malt whisky editions that are difficult to find elsewhere, whisky books, glassware, gifts and a range of other quality Scottish products.

The Centre's facilities provide a prestigious location for corporate hospitality and meetings, such as the Castlehill Room with its magnificent stained glass window depicting the history and romance of Scotch whisky, and the Blenders Room. The Centre also runs regular training courses through the Scotch Whisky Training School.

For more information contact the Centre at:
354 Castlehill, The Royal Mile,
Edinburgh EH1 2NE
Tel: (+44) 131-220-0441
Fax: (+44) 131-220-6288
Website: www.whisky-heritage.co.uk
Email: enquiry@whisky-heritage.co.uk

FLAVOUR VOCABULARY

1. BODY/WEIGHT

light, light-to-medium, medium, medium-to-full, big, bold, delicate, dense, firm, full, heavy, powerful, robust, round, weighty

2. SWEETNESS

astringent, dry, medium, medium-dry, medium-sweet, sweet

3. PEATY/SMOKEY

Smoky ash, bonfires, brimstone, burnt-sticks, cinnamon-sticks-burning, coal-gas, cordite, creosote, guaiacol, heather-peat, heather-smoke, heathery-burnt, incense, Lapsang-Souchong tea, matchboxes, molasses, oilskins, peat-reek, peaty, phenolic, pungent, rubbery, smoke-exotic, smoky, sooty, spent-fireworks, steam-engines, tar, tarred-rope, turf-burning

Kippery anchovies, dried-crab-shells, dried-shellfish, kippery sea-shells, shellfish-dried, shells-dried-crab, smoked-mussels, smoked-oysters, smoked-salmon

Mossy bracken, earthy, fishing-nets, moss-water, peat-fresh, roots, turf-fresh.

4. MEDICINAL/SALTY

Medicinal antiseptic, bath-salts, beachy, brine, Brylcreem, carbolic, diesel-oil, eucalyptus, germoline, hospitals, iodine, iron, kelp, lint, menthol, neoprene, salty, oysters ozone, sea-air, seashore, sea-spray, seaweed, surgical-spirits, TCP, turpentine

5. TOBACCO/FEINTY

Tobacco tea-chests, teapots, tobacco-aromatic, tobacco-ash, tobacco-stale

Feinty acetic, blotting-paper, bung-cloth, cardboard, cork, damp-wool,

fusty, inky, metallic, mothballs, mouldy, musty, musty-oak, old-books, paraffin, vinegar, wood-old

Leathery calf-book-binding, car-seats, cowhide, libraries, poultry-food, saddles

Sweaty buttermilk, cheesy, drains, gym-shoes-old, leather-polish, musky, piggery, shoe-polish, sickly, stale, waxed-raincoats

Plastic oilskins, plastic-buckets, plastic-mats, scorched-plastic

6. HONEY/VANILLA

Honey beeswax, honey-clover, honey-heather, honey-lavender, honey-pouring, mead

Vanilla butterscotch, cake-mix, candy-floss, caramel, cocoa-butter, cola, custard-powder, fudge, glycerine, rum-toffee, sticky-toffee-pudding, syrupy, tablet, toffee, treacle

7. SPICY/WOODY

Spicy allspice, caraway, cedar, cedarwood, chicken-masala, chilli-peppers, cigar-boxes, cinnamon, cloves, ginger, gingerbread, mustard, mustard-cress, newly-sharpened-pencils, nutmeg, oaky, pepper, pine, resinous, sandalwood, sawdust, tannic, wood-new, woody

8. WINEY/SHERRY

Sherried bourbon, brandy, burgundy, calvados, chardonnay, cider-apples, drinks-cabinet, ethereal, fino-sherry, grapey, grappa, liqueurish, madeira, manzanilla, oloroso, port, rum, sherry, spirituous, spirity, vinous, winey

9. NUTTY/CREAMY

Nutty almonds, benzaldehyde, brazil-nuts, candlewax, filbert, gun-oil, hazelnuts, lanolin, linseed-oil, marzipan, oily, olives, praline, rapeseed-oil, roasted-peanuts, unctuous, walnuts

Creamy butter, chocolate, coconuts, hand-cream, milk-chocolate, silky

10. MALTY/CEREAL

Cooked Mash agricultural, barley, biscuits, cereal-mash, draff, grain, mealy, oats, porridge, silage-sweet, Weetabix

Cooked Veg corn-boiled, potato-mashed, potato-skins-baked, swede-cooked, turnips-cooked

Malty hops, Horlicks, malt-extract, malted-milk, Marmite,

Husky bran, chaff, hops-dried, iron-tonic, pot-ale

Toasted aniseed, biscuits-digestive, bitter-chocolate, bitter-coffee, burnt, burnt-cake, burnt-toast, burnt-toffee, cocao, cake, coffee-grounds, coffee-roasted, cookies, hickory, liquorice, roasted-malt, shortbread

Yeasty baking, baking-bread, fleshy, gralloch, gravy, meaty, pork-boiled, roast-meat, sausages, venison

11. FRUITY/ESTERY

Citric ascorbic, bergamot, estery, Kiwi-fruit, lemon-sherbet, lemons, limes, mandarins, orange-rind, oranges, peel-zest, pineapple-cubes, tangerines, tart, tropical-fruit

Fresh Fruit apples, autumn-fruits, bananas, blackberries, cherries, custard-pudding, fresh-figs, fruit-green, fruit-gums, fruity, green-fruit, humbugs, lemonade, melons, peaches, pear-drops, pears, pineapples, raspberries, strawberries, sweet-shop

Cooked Fruit baked-apples, banana-rum, fruit-cooked, fruit-rotten, marmalade, plummy, prunes-stewed, raspberry-jam, stewed-apples, stewed-rhubarb

Dried Fruit apricots-dried, candy-peel, Christmas-cake, Christmas-pudding, dates, Dundee-cake, figs-dried, fruit-cake, mince-pies, peel-mixed, prunes, raisins, sultanas

Solvent American-cream-soda, bubble-gum, cellophane, ethyl-alcohol, fusil-oil, nail-varnish-remover, paint-fresh, pine-essence

12. FLORAL/HERBAL

Fragrant acetal, aromatic, barber-shop, blossom, bluebells, Earl-Grey-tea, elderflowers, floral, flowery, freesias, gentian-roses, gorse-bushes, heather, honeysuckle, lavender, lilac, marc, orange-blossom, orchards, perfumed, quinine, rhododendrons, roses, rose-water, scented, summer, violets, wet-spring-mornings

Greenhouse apple-mint, barley-sugar, bog-myrtle, boiled-sweets, carnations, flowering-currants, geraniums, green-tomatoes, mint, peppermint, sherbet, spearmint, sugared-almonds

Leafy aldehydic, coffee-green, cut-barley, cut-grass, fresh, fir-trees,green-apples, green-sticks, green-vegetables, greeny, laurel-leaves, lawn-cuttings, pea-pods, pine-cones, sappy

Herbal artichokes, barns, bayleaf, botanical, coumarin, dry-hay, fennel, grassy, green-hedgerows, harvest-fields, hay, hay-damp, heather-flowers, heathery, meadows, mulch, oregano, sage-and-onion, soap-saddle, soap-scented, straw, tea thyme

INDEX

ACKNOWLEDGEMENTS

The following have been especially helpful in giving advice and encouragement Bobby Anderson, Pamela van Ankeren, Raymond Armstrong, Helen Arthur, Elaine Bailey, Rachel Barrie, William Bergius, Steve Blake, Neil Boyd, Erich Braun, Jake Bremner, Neil Cameron, John Campbell, George Christie, Isabel Coughlin, David Cox, Bob Dalgarno, Ed Dodson, Gavin Durnin, Leslie Duroe, Graham Eunson, Marion Ferguson, Robert Fleming, Derek Gilchrist, John L. S. Grant, Alan Greig, Glen Gribbon, Robert Hay, Iain Henderson, Robert Hicks, Fraser Hughes, Christine Jones, Richard Joynson, David King, John Lamond, Ronnie Learmond, Paul Lobar, René Looper, Bill Lumsden, William McCallum, Tom McCulloch, Jim McEwan, Frank McHardy, Alastair McIntosh, Douglas MacKay, Nicola Mackinlay, Charles MacLean, John MacLellan, Ian MacMillan, Duncan McNicoll, Ita McShannon, Graham MacWilliam, Dennis Malcolm, Theo Metzger, Ian Miller, Douglas Milne, Wallace Milroy, Euan Mitchell, Susan Morrison, Gordon Motion, Norma Munro, Richard Paterson, David Quinn, John Ramsay, Michael Ray, John Reid, Graeme Richardson, Alastair Robertson, David Robertson, Colin Ross, Freda Ross, Innes Shaw, Andrew Sinclair, Derek Sinclair, Fred Sinclair, Stuart Smith, Mitchell Sorbie, Jacqui Stacey, Gordon Steele, David Stewart, Keir Sword, Andrew Symington, William Tait, Yvonne Thackeray, Jackie and Stuart Thomson, HRH The Prince of Wales, Malcolm Waring and Alan Winchester. Thanks also to those distillers and producers who have generously supported *Whisky Classified* seminars and tutored tastings.
I would also like to acknowledge the assistance of Allied Distillers Ltd, Angus Dundee Distillers Plc, Bacardi & Co. Ltd, Ben Nevis Distillery Ltd, Berry Bros & Rudd Ltd, Bruichladdich Distillery Co. Ltd, Burn Stewart Distillers Plc, Old Bushmills Distillery Co. Ltd, Chivas Bros. Ltd, Cutty Sark International, Diageo Plc, Delhaize "Le Lion" s.a., John Dewar & Sons Ltd, The Edrington Group, Glenmorangie Plc, Gordon & MacPhail Ltd, J & G Grant, William Grant and Sons Ltd, Highland Distillers Ltd, Isle of Arran Distillers Ltd, Inver House Distillers, Kyndal International Plc, Loch Lomond Distillery Co. Ltd, J & A Mitchell & Co. Ltd, Morrison Bowmore Distillers Ltd, Royal Mile Whiskies, Scotch Malt Whisky Society, Scotch Whisky Association, Scotch Whisky Heritage Centre, Scotch Whisky Research Institute, Speyside Distillery Co. Ltd, Tomatin Distillery Co. Ltd and WhiskyShip Zurich.

Lastly, I would like to thank my Publisher, Vivien James; my Designer, Bernard Higton; my two patient Editors, Nina Sharman and Jessica Spencer; Head of Publicity, Anne O'Neill; Photographer, Douglas Robertson; Editorial Assistant, Mary Macnaghten; University Press Officer, Claire Grainger; the man who set me up for this, Colin Webb; and my wife Doreen Wishart, for all the help and support she has given to me over the past 5 years.

PICTURE CREDITS

Allied Distillers Ltd. pp.9 bottom, 41, 160, 186; Ben Nevis Distillery Ltd.; Berry Bros & Rudd Ltd. p.15; Bladnoch Distillery p.76 top; The Bridgeman Art Library p.12; Bruichladdich Distillery Company Ltd. pp.19, 23, 26 top, 38 top, 41 bottom, 82; Burn Stewart Distillers pp.102 both, 206; Campbell Distillers Ltd. pp.106, 108; Chivas Brothers Ltd. pp.18 bottom, 20 bottom, 70, 126 top, 128, 166, 194; Chrysalis Images pp.14 bottom, 20 top, 21 top, 31; David Wishart pp.9 top, 44, 46, 52, 56 bottom, 64, 66, 76 bottom, 78 both, 94, 96, 100, 104, 114, 124 bottom, 126 bottom, 130, 132, 142, 156, 172, 174, 196, 202, 208, 210, 212, 214; The Edrington Group p.124; Glenmorangie Plc. pp.2 bottom left, 8, 25, 40, 50, 136, 138; Gordon & MacPhail p.74; Diageo Plc. pp.1 top left, 5, 10, 16, 21 bottom, 58, 72, 86, 88, 90, 92, 116, 134, 140, 146, 152, 158, 162, 170, 176, 184, 198, 204; Highland Distillers Ltd. pp.84, 148, 150, 200 both; Inver House Distillers pp.14, 48, 62, 180, 188; Isle of Arran Distillers p.54; J & G Grant p.118 both; John Dewar & Sons Ltd. pp.110, 182; Johnny MacKinnon p.144; Kyndal Spirits Ltd. pp.98, 154, 178; Kintyre Photography p.192; Loch Lomond Distillery p.164 bottom; www.loch-lomond.net p.164 top; The Macallan Distillers Ltd. pp.17, 29, 168; Morrison Bowmore Distillers Ltd. pp.18 top, 22, 32, 39, 56 top, 80, 122; The Speyside Distillery Archive and Klim Design Inc. p.190; Strathview Photographic, p.60; V & A Picture Library p.11; William Grant & Sons pp.7, 24, 28, 120.
Photographs of whisky bottles by Douglas Robertson and pp.6, 25 bottom, 26 bottom, 30, 33, 35 both, 36, 37.

Technical Reference

Wishart, D., Classification of Single Malt Whiskies, In: Data Analysis, Classification and Related Methods, Springer, Berlin, 2000, p.89–94.
www.clustan.com and www.whiskyclassified.com